Don't stop at the lights

Leading your church through a changing climate

Dedication

To our endlessly supportive and understanding spouses,
Jacqui Shreeve and David Foster

Don't stop at the lights

Leading your church through a changing climate

Claire Foster and David Shreeve

CHURCH HOUSE PUBLISHING

Church House Publishing
Church House
Great Smith Street
London
SW1P 3AZ

Tel: 020 7898 1451
Fax: 020 7898 1449

ISBN   978 0 7151 4138 0

Published 2008 by Church House Publishing

The opinions expressed in this book are those of the authors and do not necessarily
reflect the official policy of the General Synod or The Archbishops' Council of the
Church of England.

Design & typesetting by Penguin Boy Ltd.   www.penguinboy.net
Illustrations by Simon Oxley.   www.idokungfoo.com

Printed in England by Ashford Colour Press Ltd, Gosport, Hampshire
on recycled paper made from 100% post-consumer waste

Contents

Foreword

Every year London clergy meet together in St Paul's Cathedral on Maundy Thursday to share in Holy Communion and to recall the new commandment of Jesus Christ that we are 'to love one another as he has loved us'.

At the end of the service the holy oils are distributed, but this year each priest also received an energy-saving light bulb. In modern circumstances it is not possible to be serious about neighbour love without reflecting on the impact that our style of life is having on the lives of those least able to adapt to the fact of climate change and rising sea levels. Cutting the carbon and reducing our energy consumption is one of the ways of recognizing the interdependence of all those who live on our beautiful planet.

There is much that we can do relatively painlessly and swiftly – hence the light bulbs. But, listening to the debates around the passage of the Climate Change Bill through Parliament, I have become aware that the moral imperative to share resources more equitably among the people of the earth will have a profound impact on every part of our lives. There will have to be a spiritual revolution if the necessary changes are to be made without damaging social disruption. We have to recover a joyful sense that we are creatures, participants in a web of life, whose health depends on the health of others, rather than masters and possessors of the world.

This book assembles resources for use in church and privately throughout the year. Claire Foster and David Shreeve, drawing on years of work in the field, have collected stories and ideas from across the world to help us shrink our footprint and reboot our world view. They offer us not just tips on energy saving but a reorientation. There is more matter here than in books twice the size. The intention is not to urge Christians to get measured for a hair shirt but to rediscover 'how good and joyful a thing it is to dwell together in unity' with all that lives.

Richard Chartres
Bishop of London
World Ocean Day 2008

Acknowledgements

The authors and publishers would like to thank the following people for their contributions to and feedback on the manuscript:

Dr Margaret Barker, Rt Revd Dr Richard Chartres, Revd Barry Goodwin, Revd Dr Christopher Jones, Revd Jeanne Males, Revd Helen Marshall, Revd Peter Moger, Father Kevin Morris, Father Robert Murray SJ, Revd Ian White.

The authors and publisher gratefully acknowledge permission to reproduce copyright material in this book. Every effort has been made to trace and contact copyright holders. If there are any inadvertent omissions we apologize to those concerned and will ensure that a suitable acknowledgement is made in all future editions.

The hymn 'God in his love for us lent us this planet' by Fred Pratt Green is copyright © Stainer & Bell Ltd, London, England, 1973 and reproduced by permission (p. 16).

Ali Newell, Confession from *The Iona Abbey Worship Book*, copyright © The Iona Community, 2001. Reproduced by permission (pp. 16–17).

'The unmaking of the world' by Naomi Mara Hyman is from *Torah of the Earth Vol. 2: Exploring 4,000 Years of Ecology* in Jewish Thought, copyright © 2000. Edited by Arthur Waskow. Permission granted by Jewish Lights Publishing, P.O. Box 237, Woodstock, VT 05091 *www.jewishlights.com* (pp. 18–19).

Extract from *Copenhagen* by Michael Frayn, published by Methuen Drama, an imprint of A&C Black Publishers Ltd. Reproduced by permission (pp. 19–20).

Additional Collect for Pentecost (p. 21), Blessing for Plough Sunday (p. 40) and Prayer for use at the offering of incense (p. 45) from *Common Worship: Times and Seasons*, copyright © The Archbishops' Council, 2006.

Introduction

Introduction

Why should concern for the environment concern Christians? Is it just a popular bandwagon to jump on because the headlines are growing louder every day? Is it just another secular concern that troubles us because it troubles our world, but nothing more than that? Should the Church keep its hands off, and leave the solutions to the scientists and politicians? Or is the degradation of our environment at base a spiritual issue? Are the consumer culture and the modern project of growth without limit, which have at least partly contributed to the growing crisis, products of a society that has lost its spiritual roots? To put it another way, if our society were to reconnect with its spiritual roots, would that help the environment? Or, more contentiously, has Christian theology to bear some of the blame for human behaviour?

This book has been written on the understanding that there is a profound Christian theological basis for environmental concern. Exploring the roots of our faith with care for the planet in mind stirs up new growth, new inspiration and new practical engagements for Christian churches. It also gives a distinctively Christian spiritual contribution to contemporary environmental discourse that is much appreciated in social, political, regulatory and grassroots circles, and is welcomed by other faiths that are also awake to the call of environmental concern.

The reality of environmental degradation has also challenged us to re-examine Christian scriptures and traditions with open minds and an attitude of humility. For Christian thinking has not been blameless. But in seeking to soften some traditions, we have found that others, just as old, just as biblical, have come into sharper focus. Everything is refreshed, and we discover we are elucidating very new and very old truths from our Christian storehouse.

Don't stop at the lights . . .

This book follows on from our previous title *How Many Lightbulbs Does It Take to Change a Christian?*[1] It is inspired by the realization that changing our light bulbs is only the first step on a journey. On its own, changing a light bulb will not save the earth. But the very act of changing one thing opens up the possibility of deepening and broadening our understanding of how to care for creation.

This book aims to energize you and inspire you to:
- Study Christian scriptures and tradition.
- Look again at the creation.
- Undertake silent contemplation.
- Preach with energy and commitment.
- Use your church as a beacon in the community.
- Energize your congregations and multiply your own enthusiasm, through them, out into their own homes and the communities of which they are members.

The shape of this book

We have taken the Christian year as the framework for the book in the hope that the thoughts offered here will fit into the world that clergy and other church leaders occupy and have to service, day by day, week by week, season by season.

The material for each season includes:
- an opening summary of the overarching theme, the practical suggestions and the theological themes;
- an introduction;
- practical ideas: a mixture of liturgical suggestions, practical tips and case studies to inspire you;
- study notes: an in-depth exploration of

theological themes;

- sermon points: suggestions for use in your teaching;
- liturgical links: suggested material for use in worship.

The practical ideas are often taken from historical Church practices. Many of these have rural associations because until relatively recently much of the Church was in rural areas, but we also recommend them for urban churches. Disconnection from the natural world underlies much of our environmental malpractice and following these ideas may help congregations reconnect both with the land where our food comes from, and with the roots of our Christian rituals.

The theological ideas that have been related to the Christian festivals and seasons are also rooted in ancient ideas. They are substantially influenced by Old Testament scholar Margaret Barker's work on Temple theology and they, too, should reconnect congregations with the roots of their faith, evoking new ways of thinking about the old stories.

Both the practical and theological ideas relate the rhythm of the year to the environment we all share. Although the actions and study guides are linked to specific seasons of the Church year, there is no reason not to pick up a theme at another time of year – when, for example, there may be more time to study a theological point in greater depth, or for your congregation to get involved in some activity.

Ideally, this book should be read in conjunction with *How Many Lightbulbs Does It Take to Change a Christian?*, which has hundreds of ecological ideas for individuals. Another publication, *For Creed and Creation*, contains the information needed for a church to run itself in an ecologically friendly way, and this, too, is recommended for priests and ministers.[2]

Acknowledging the challenges

If we were building churches today, it is unlikely that we would be creating anything like the buildings we have inherited. While a few may conform to today's building and environmental requirements, we know that many of those built even a handful of years ago fail to meet current standards, so how can those built four hundred years ago or more ever be deemed 'environment friendly'?

And here is just one of our challenges – we are using buildings totally devoid of energy efficiency where the words of Ezekiel are more likely to be quoted than those of the Energy Saving Trust, and where terms such as low-level lighting, efficient heating and basic insulation may be as remote today as they were unknown in the past. We are dealing with a world of apses, aisles and flying buttresses created when Black and Decker were a far distant song and dance act and carbon sequestration would have beaten all but the most distinguished of Latin scholars.

But before we simply knock everything down and start again, just consider another person's point of view. Not the Sunday worshipper, but one of the many who come, provided the church is open or the key is handy, to visit out of interest, fascination and sometimes simply pure love. Here is a place of atmosphere by the yard, where history is not just real, it's there to touch, to smell, to feel. Where memorials and tablets tell of times past, of honours, of lives lived and things that are still to come – this is our heritage, and it is just as important a part of conservation as switching off the lights and servicing the boiler. Worshippers may complain about the state of affairs – the bills, the draughts, the Archdeacon's visitation, but the rest, who may well be the majority, want preservation. Faith, hope and continuity are what is needed, but how does the bell keep ringing when the only things in the place that are protected are the bats?

Everyone knows the environmental issues facing the world and many will ask what possible effect a lonely parish church can have on the great picture. But conservation is all about everyone taking responsibility for the planet and about everyone, including the church, playing their part. The following pages will give a range of ideas of how. It could be saving energy, or increasing biodiversity; it could be recycling; it could simply be about setting an example and doing something that relates to today's world.

Where do we start?

When we hear people say they know what the issues are but don't know what to do, we are amazed because so much information is available. And furthermore very little of it is new. Perhaps there is too much. David's mum used to save paper bags and his dad used to shout, 'Who's left that light on?' They never described themselves as 'environmentalists' but they had to watch the pennies. So do most churches. So much of the advice about energy saving can also be 'money saving'. But as with many good things, there is a price to pay: new bulbs — and that can sometimes mean new fittings; a new efficient boiler — and more often than not that has been put off for several years; and then there's insulation, draught proofing and

always someone who suggests putting solar panels on the south-facing roof. Where do we begin?

As with anything else in the church, success comes because an individual has taken up the challenge. You may want to consider how to get others on board, how to motivate your whole congregation. One way is to use some of the ideas in this book to inspire your preaching and teaching. Alongside this, you may want to plan a year's worth of environmental action, using some of the practical suggestions given here. You don't have to do it all yourself. Perhaps a keen member of the congregation might act as an environmental champion.

It's worth thinking about publicizing what you are doing, too. Churches can be beacons in their communities. Might the local press be interested in a particular initiative, such as a churchyard clear-up or development of a garden — or even some new solar panels? Can you use notice boards (both internal and external) to share news and pictures of what you are doing?

It's also worth considering how to involve all ages. Children and young people often have a great concern for the environment and the enthusiasm to do some-

FIFTY THINGS THAT COULD SAVE THE PLANET

In 2007 the UK's Environment Agency asked 25 environmentalists, from businesses, NGOs, the media, think tanks and its own organization: 'What are the 50 things that really could save the planet?' Announcing the results, Sir John Harman, the then chairman of the Agency, commented: 'They are a revelation. A genuine mix of the political, technological, philosophical, social and domestic. There are plenty of things you'd expect to be in there, but not necessarily where you'd expect to find them. And there are some surprises, too.'

And he was right, for in second position, between number 1: 'Powering down' — reducing our electricity use, and number 3: 'Sun worshipping' — harnessing energy from the sun, was: 'A leap of faith' — religious leaders need to make the planet their priority.

Nick Reeves, Executive Director of the Chartered Institute of Water and the Environment (CIWEM), commented: 'It is time the world's faith groups reminded us that we have a duty to restore and maintain the ecological balance of the planet.'

thing about it. The older generation may have much wisdom to share, from practical tips for recycling through to skills and crafts and knowledge of local folklore. Concern for the environment affects and should involve the whole worshipping community.

Help from the wider Church

An instruction from General Synod, which in 2005 debated the report *Sharing God's Planet* asked for a report by 2008 on how a measured reduction in energy consumption of the Church of England could be achieved.[3] The Synod called upon the whole Church at every level to engage with the issues of climate change and energy use.

Following on from this instruction, and as a further step forward in the campaign to 'green' the Church, the Church of England marked World Environment Day 2006 (Monday 5 June) by launching **Shrinking the Footprint** with the initial aim of **Measuring our Footprint**. All those responsible for parish churches, diocesan offices and bishops' houses were asked to carry out an audit of energy used in 2005 so that a benchmark could be established. The size of the 'carbon footprint' having been assessed, Shrinking the Footprint would roll out initiatives and encouragement to reduce energy use in a variety of ways.

All Diocesan Environmental Officers received an audit pack to undertake 'Measuring our Footprint' assessments of current levels and types of energy consumption in church buildings in every parish. Churches were also invited to promote discussion of the issues.

The audit resources were issued electronically to keep paper consumption to a minimum.[4]

Don't Stop at the Lights marks the next stage in the campaign. The Church is working with the Carbon Trust and the Energy Saving Trust to examine examples of its wide-ranging properties, including clergy houses, so that footprints can be reduced in a variety of ways.

Why it matters: public spirituality

Concern for the environment obliges religion to be public – there is nothing more public, more shared, than our planet. But just beating a drum, although important, will not be enough for clergy, who have to sustain themselves and their congregations over the long term. Jordi Pigem said:

> When a passionate concern for the world is not nurtured by spiritual insight, it often leads to despair or burn-out ... External, material resources diminish the more they are used. But our best inner resources grow and are replenished the more we get them out, the more we extend them to reach others.[5]

God is the only clean, limitless source of energy we have.

Surely Sir John Harman's words (see the box on page 4) are a call we cannot afford to ignore. We hope that this book will help you.

Claire Foster and David Shreeve

PS: While this first edition of *Don't Stop at the Lights* contains many practical examples, the authors are aware that there could be many more. If you can supply details of projects, initiatives or campaigns for a future edition, please send them to David Shreeve, Mission and Public Affairs, Church House, Great Smith Street, London, SW1P 3AZ, email: *david.shreeve@c-of-e.org.uk*

Advent

Overarching theme:
Acknowledging the power and force of the creation and humanity's role in harming it.

Practical themes:
- Planning an environmental audit
- Nature studies
- Taking stock: decluttering
- Letting the light shine

Theological themes:
- Advent as a time of uncertainty and hope
- The sea as a metaphor for power and chaos
- Environmental degradation expressed as 'world upside down'
- Renewal as a possibility, however bad things become

Introduction

Advent as a time of expectation holds the coming of the kingdom in threefold anticipation: the coming of the kingdom at the end of time; the coming of the kingdom as the Christ child; the coming of the kingdom now, here, among us.[1] It is a dark time in the Church calendar, a time of withdrawal and absence, in sharp contrast to the bright lights of the High Street where the Christmas season starts all too early.

The essence of Advent is anticipation, and this speaks to our environmental situation. An individual looks at the findings of the Intergovernmental Panel on Climate Change (IPCC) and is faced with the terrifying global consequences of continuing the human project of economic growth. We are conscious of the desire in ourselves to carry on as if nothing was happening, because for the time being I can afford to, because my government is making no demands on me to restrain my consumption patterns, because international agreements don't yet impinge on my lifestyle choices … because if I don't carry on as if nothing was happening, if I face up to the IPCC findings, I might despair. But Advent prods me to face reality, and to hope.

Advent is a good time to realize the significance of climate change because the mindset for this season is one of 'living on the edge': in our spiritual lives and our liturgy, Advent is when we are without our Saviour, only anticipating him. Our world disintegrates around us; social unrest is everywhere; human beings quarrel and hurt one another while the earth burns up. We have no idea how to reverse the diabolical (literally: falling apart, dividing up) trend. Advent brings hope of a totally new event that will change everything so that nothing will look the same again. But it is not a done deal. We hope, but we are not certain. We are living on the edge.

Our hope is that what seems unavoidable because of the seemingly unbreakable laws of cause and effect will be overturned. In today's context, the devastat-ing effects of climate change seem inevitable. In the Advent season we revisit in our imaginations this same dull despair, before Christ comes and changes everything. Einstein's physics have evoked the possibility of uncertainty and change in the face of seemingly unchangeable laws of nature. At the heart of events, something totally new can appear. A germ of a new order, present in random activity, can become a 'strange attractor', breaking symmetry. This can produce a novelty that is unpredictable and sometimes stunningly beautiful, reorganizing the whole system and working against the forces of destruction.

One such 'strange attractor' was the seemingly impossible emergence of the blue-green algae that first created a breathable atmosphere on earth. In a completely different way, but just as seemingly impossible, was the birth of a vulnerable human being who was to be the saviour of the world. What strange attractor may even now turn the mind of the human family away from self-destruction, and the earth away from its predicted hot, steady state — in which the actions and reactions triggering catastrophic environmental changes cause the temperature of the earth to rise fast, and eventually settle at a much higher level, where only the two poles and some islands are habitable by people and most creatures?[2]

Liturgy can be used to express the chaos and drama of 'living on the edge'. In Shakespeare's plays, as things become more chaotic and dramatic, the language becomes more formal, often moving from prose to blank verse, not to reduce the power of the chaos, but to express it. The formality of the verse makes expression possible. It is notable that at times of great mourning, such as a loved one's funeral, the form of the funeral service can express the inarticulate cry of loss that people feel and cannot speak. Liturgy can be similarly used to express the descent into chaos promised by speeded up climate change.

Practical ideas for Advent

Colour: purple but sometimes blue[3]

Advent is one of the longest periods of the Christian year, but it is shorter now than it was in the past, when it started on St Martin's Day, 11 November. This section of the handbook is consequently longer than most of the other sections, with more theology and a larger number of practical suggestions.

In environmental terms, the essence of Advent is anticipation and hope. In the northern hemisphere, it is easy to think of Advent as a time of expectancy, for the world around us is dormant. In the southern hemisphere, by contrast, Christmas lunch often involves a barbecue on the beach. We have to remember that, despite what our shopping bags may tell us, there still are seasons of the year and on the other side of the world Advent is full of late spring flowers, early summer forest fires and drought.

Just as the cosmic web includes opposite seasons, so it contains opposing environmental forces and concerns. The by-pass that will take the traffic out of the village centre will pass through someone's sacred space, and the wind turbine will turn a favourite view into a power station.

Time to reflect and plan

Advent is the time when the Church renews her service; it is the beginning of the ecclesiastical year – the reason why, says Wheatley, the Church does not number her days nor measure her seasons by the motion of the sun is because she follows the course of our Saviour who, as the true sun of righteousness, began now to rise upon the world.[4]

This, then, if it has not already been done, would be a good time to start **planning an environmental audit**.

Nature studies

Climates may see changes and nature may be fooled into waking early, but to the theologians, the poets and the carollers, Advent will probably remain the

---

ENVIRONMENTAL AUDITS

For the Church of England's 'Shrinking the Footprint' Energy Audit for churches and church buildings, see Appendix 5. Church audits can also be found at:

www.arcworld.org
www.christian-ecology.org.uk
www.ew.ecocongregation.org

The audit should involve the whole of the church, its buildings and its land in order to produce a 'green-print' for the new year ahead. Now will be a time when draughts will be easy to locate and you will know whether last year's problem with the boiler really was just an air-lock or something rather more serious.

time when the world is sleeping, waiting for new life. And so it is a great time for teaching. In the northern hemisphere, the birds may have flown away, but we can plant bulbs and look forward. One vicar, keen to teach his young flock how to read, planted snowdrops in the shape of letters in the churchyard. Not only did the youngsters spend Advent peering for the first signs of new life, but they had learned their ABC by the time the snowdrops were in full flower. Today, of course, learning in such a way would be considered far too laborious, but teaching using the magic of nature does hold a certain charm and mystery and can lead to a lifetime's fascination and appreciation of plants and living things and wonderment at God's creation.

Advent's own tree

There is a tree associated with Advent, but it's no ordinary tree and does not grow in the usual places, for it is only found in paintings, carvings and stained-glass windows.

The Jesse tree and its origins are found in Isaiah 11.1-2:

> *A shoot shall come out from the stock of Jesse, and a branch shall grow out of his roots. The spirit of the LORD shall rest on him, the spirit of wisdom and understanding, the spirit of counsel and might, the spirit of knowledge and the fear of the LORD.*

The Jesse tree can be used as a focus in the Church during Advent, through Christmas and beyond into Epiphany. There is an excellent history of the Jesse tree and suggestions on how to incorporate it into a church's Advent programme and services in *Together for a Season*.[5]

The Advent wreath

Just when the custom of the **Advent wreath** began is, like many such customs, a mystery. The wreath comprises a circle of evergreen, signifying continuous life, on which there are five candles, four on the circle,

and one in the middle. The candles represent hope, love, joy, peace and Christmas. On the first Sunday in Advent, the first candle is lit, and an additional candle is lit on each of the following Sundays. On Christmas Day, the central candle is lit, so that now all five candles are burning. The wreath, having no beginning or end, symbolizes the eternity of God.

> *O come, O Dayspring, come and cheer*
> *Our spirits by thine advent here*
> *And drive away the shades of night*
> *And pierce the clouds and bring us light.*
>
> Author unknown
> translated from the eighth-century Latin
> by J. M. Neale

Taking stock and showing off

Advent is also the time to take stock and consider the clutter that may have accumulated in and around the church. Are there some things that are not needed and could be recycled for others to use? It is also a time to consider the churchyard or the garden. Can anything be done there to clear clutter and address renewal?

Let the light shine!

And what about those who may not have an awareness of what Advent means? Could each step of the gradual build up to Christmas be marked by **one token floodlight** on part of the church, beginning on Advent Sunday and gradually increasing to full floodlighting of the building for Christmas Eve? This could become a wonderful illuminated Advent calendar for everyone in your parish to share. This idea was suggested by the authors to the environment group of Grafton Cathedral in New South Wales just before Advent 2007 and the idea was immediately taken up, with full coverage in the local media.

At the same time, you could extend the idea of the Advent calendar to create a plan for the coming year with the calendar's 'windows' featuring environmental tasks and opportunities for every month, or even every week!

THE VALUE OF NATURE

What price do we put on nature? A painting of a landscape, tree or flower can be worth millions of pounds, but what about the real thing? Many churches have an ancient yew tree growing nearby. Some trees are estimated to be a thousand years old or more. How much is their heritage worth?

When the University of Texas was building a new dormitory recently, a sign was hung nearby declaring: 'Do not discard or pour paint, mortar, trash or any construction materials or debris on this tree. The replacement value of this oak tree is $90,000.' A tree census in New York City valued the city's nearly 600,000 trees at $122 million. A rough breakdown: $11 million for filtering out air pollutants, $28 million saved in energy consumption (less need for air conditioners), $36 million in aesthetic benefits.

So how much value would you put on the trees in your churchyard or community? This would be an interesting exercise for all the congregation to undertake – especially at this time of the year when people are only too aware of the price of Christmas trees, which only last a couple of weeks.

To estimate the age of a churchyard yew, contact:

The Conservation Foundation at ***www.conservationfoundation.co.uk***

The Ancient Yew Group at ***www.ancient-yew.org***

LITURGICAL LINKS

- See *Common Worship: Times and Seasons*, pages 33–60 (also at **www.cofe.anglican.org/worship/liturgy/commonworship/texts**). This resource includes prayers and penitential material for use at the Advent wreath.
- Further suggestions for using an Advent wreath in worship can be found in *Together for a Season*, volume 1.
- For a sequence of readings on the theme of light at an Advent carol service, see *Common Worship: Times and Seasons*.
- Further resources are available in *The Carol Book*.[7]

Study notes and sermon points for Advent

Advent as a time of uncertainty and expectation can be an opportunity to realize how alive and unpredictable the universe can be: how, whether we perceive it or not, we are living on the edge.

Living on the edge 1: The sea

STUDY NOTES

Creation is a good deal more powerful and frightening than we sometimes think. Those of us lucky enough to be protected against the worst of the elements are shocked into a realization of their power when floods, hurricanes and droughts hit our mostly tidy lives. Advent is a good time to become aware of this power as we anticipate Christ's coming, he whom even the winds and waves obeyed. Because of its immense size and wildness, the sea is an emblem of the mighty forces of creation. It may not be domesticated.

The powerful elements are bound by God's eternal covenant

God's covenant with creation, made with Noah and all living things, binds the forces of nature to God: Genesis 9.8-10. The power of the cosmic elements, including the supernatural creatures, which do not appear in the Genesis creation story, and the binding force of the covenant in which they are all involved, is a recurring theme in the Old Testament: for example, Psalm 74.12-14. By referring to the historical event of the exodus from Egypt, Second Isaiah proclaims the power of God to change those boundaries at will: Isaiah 51.9-11. First Isaiah projects the overcoming of the Leviathan sea monster into eschatological time: Isaiah 27.1. Job is shown the mighty works of God in the finely observed chapters 38 and 39, including the binding of the waters: Job 38.8-11. In Jeremiah 5.22, the sand is the barrier to the sea, the text offering a juxtaposition of flatness and passivity against roaring might.

The reader is struck by the power that is demonstrated. The sea does indeed roar and, for the most part, the waves unceasingly crash on to the shore without transgressing the bounds of the sand. To the onlooker, the endless bounded power is fascinating because such potency and vigour hold transgression in ever present potential. The liveliness of the covenant is enhanced by the thought of the chaos that would ensue if the potential were ever realized: Jeremiah 5.22. It's a harrowing image for the twenty-first-century reader thinking of rising sea levels and their threat to coastal habitats.

God restores the earth

In Psalm 104, a similar description of the covenant is given but here, rather than creation, its quality is of restoration following the flood. The promise is that the waters 'might not again cover the earth', and the vigour of the elements is re-emphasized. But the power of God is thereby stressed even more, and the dormant, terrifying chaos is recalled to mind: Psalm 104.5-9.

Advent and the sea

Advent calls Christian disciples to open their minds and hearts to the powerful potential of the time:

God is now and not quite yet. Advent is living on the edge of chaos: terrifying, but honest, clear-sighted, and full of the possibility of renewal and change. In her essay 'No more sea', the eco-feminist theologian Catherine Keller points out the absolute resistance of Job's Leviathan to domestication and commodification (Job 41.5b–7a).[8] She gives us five characteristics of the untameable ocean motif that speak to our present-day planetary concerns.

First is the characteristic of non-predictability and nonlinearity. Keller quotes Paul Davies, physicist: 'Chaos seems to provide a bridge between the deterministic laws of physics and the laws of chance, implying that the universe is genuinely creative.'[9] We have a divine promise of redemption in Christ, but this is not the same as being able to predict what is going to happen to us or the universe. In the same way, if I hold a stick directly upright on my palm and let it go, it could fall in any direction. Gravity is unbiased. But the stick *will* fall in one direction and once it has done that, a train of actions will follow that will be different from those that would have taken place if the stick had fallen in a different way. So it is with every movement in creation.

Secondly, there is radical interrelation between absolutely everything. The relation is not random but functions in a dynamic web of intermeshed causal processes. Everything affects and is affected by everything else. This moment now is unique. It is caused by everything that has gone before, and it will affect everything that follows.

Thirdly, there is criticality. Try the sand-pile experiment: pile up dry sand as high as you can, and see how at a certain unpredictable point just one more grain of sand will cause the whole pile to collapse. After the pile has fallen it's possible to calculate what happened and to see that the experiment followed laws of nature, but that critical point could not have been predicted ahead of time. Criticality is frightening in relation to the environment — just one more aero-plane in the air or one more power station could be the straw that breaks the camel's back, forcing the earth to shoot into a hot, steady state, destroying most habitats. But criticality also brings hope — there may be a point when one more mind and heart changing to be concerned about the environment, or one more tiny action to help the environment, may be the one movement that turns the destruction around.

Fourthly, Keller speaks of self-similarity in relationships, which are never between two hermetically-sealed separate entities. She calls relationship an 'intersubjective filigree' that includes all other subjects. Everything in the universe is a subject, nothing is an object, and as Lucy Winkett has said: 'There's no them and us, there's only us.'[10] The 'us' includes all creatures, not just human beings. The other cannot be kept outside myself and it is always multiple. Jeffrey Sachs, economic adviser to the UN, has said that the challenge of our time is to realize there is no 'them' to fight or blame for ecological problems. We are all architects both of our destruction and our redemption.

Finally, Keller describes our existence as being always on the edge of chaos. Chaos cannot be defeated by order. The 'rich, indeterminate edges of spatio-temporality brim with potential cosmos'.[11] The ruach, the breath, of Genesis 1.2 hovers, vibrates, precisely at that edge, upon that face of the deep. Life evolves to the edge of chaos. Keller says:

> The sustaining of the great wealth of species, of biodiversity and of cultural diversity, at the same time provokes a bottomless love — a love for that endlessly rotting and renewing riot of life of which we are a clever and troublesome bit. And love is its own reward, needing no final prize.[12]

SERMON POINTS

- The image of the seemingly untameable ocean works to convey the power of God but also respect from humans.
- The critical moment that brings about terrible destruction or wonderful renewal could be this next moment. The 'chaos theory' means we cannot predict when that will be.
- Life at the edge means great potential in the heart of despair.

Living on the edge 2: World upside down

STUDY NOTES

As everything is bound together, the destruction of the covenant affects everything

In the covenant's 'loosened state' when the people relaxed their hold on their side of the covenant, the consequences could be described as a 'world upside down'.[14]

Isaiah 24 describes the terrifying effect of the loosening of the covenant, and in so doing indicates all the elements of this covenant and their connected effects. The poetry, in its threefold symmetry, and its linking of the human condition with the natural and the supernatural, serves to emphasize the interdependence of all the elements. Note, too, that the Lord starts the destructive ball rolling: Isaiah 24.1-3. Here we read of the equality of destiny faced alike by all people, whoever they are, whatever their occupation. This is one of the curious and noteworthy characteristics of the cosmic covenant. Since all parts affect all parts, as it were, there can be no individualized blame for wrongdoing. If there is drought, everyone, good and bad, suffers.

Modern responses to such 'natural disasters' are that they are, first, nobody's fault and therefore impersonal, nothing to do with us, something to be suffered and incapable of being affected by the individual; and, second, indications of the non-existence of a (good) God. In contrast to such separation of human and natural events, the world view of the cosmic covenant, with its interlinking of all elements, puts a responsibility on to all those elements, the natural and the supernatural, as well as the human. Such mutual responsibility is

THE COVENANT

The biblical scholar Robert Murray coined the phrase 'cosmic covenant' and explains it thus. The cosmic covenant focuses on the biblical evidence for a belief that ancient Israel shared with neighbouring cultures, one well documented especially from Egypt and Mesopotamia: the belief in a divinely willed order harmoniously linking heaven and earth. In Israelite tradition this was established at creation, when the cosmic elements were fixed and bound to maintain the order; but the harmony was broken and permanently threatened by disorderly supernatural beings and forces, hostile to God and to humankind. The myth of the Flood and subsequent re-creation, at which in some texts (Genesis 9; Isaiah 54.9-10) God promised his 'eternal covenant' with all creatures, expressed the belief that the cosmic harmony was the will of YHWH; but, for Israel as for her neighbours, it had to be preserved in face of hostile forces. Human collaboration in this task was effected by maintaining justice with mercy and by ritual actions, in which kings play the leading part.[13]

entirely appropriate to the twenty-first century, in which the greatest threats are equally cosmic, from global terrorism to the prospect of an overheated planet taking extraordinary measures to reduce its own temperature. We know, for example, that though the 2004 tsunami was due to natural causes, its destructive force was due to coastal development.

The ancients evolved responses to the world turning upside down in the form of Temple rituals, especially the annual ritual of atonement. Such responses remain appropriate today. In our liturgy we can give formal, communal expression to penitence for harm done, knowingly or unknowingly, for greed and exclusivity, for thoughtlessness, and we can offer prayers for strength to change and restore the damage.

Some suggestions are:

1   A reading from Isaiah chapter 24:

The earth dries up and withers,
the world languishes and withers;
the heavens languish together with the earth.
The earth lies polluted under its inhabitants;
for they have transgressed laws,
violated the statutes,
broken the everlasting covenant.
Therefore a curse devours the earth,
and its inhabitants suffer for their guilt;
therefore the inhabitants of the earth dwindled,
and few people are left.

Isaiah 24.4–6

2   Shakespeare's poem, 'Blow, blow thou winter wind'. This was sung at St Paul's Cathedral as part of an environmental service focusing on the atmosphere:

Blow, blow thou winter wind
Thou art not so unkind
As man's ingratitude;
Thy tooth is not so keen
Because thou art not seen
Although thy breath be rude.

Heigh-ho! sing heigh-ho! unto the green holly:
Most friendship is feigning, most loving mere folly:
Then heigh-ho! the holly! This life is most jolly.

Freeze, freeze thou bitter sky,
That dost not bite so nigh
As benefits forgot:
Though thou the waters warp,
Thy sting is not so sharp
As friend remembered not.

William Shakespeare

3   The following hymn, which was sung at the opening worship of a clergy study day on environmental issues:

God in his love for us lent us this planet,
Gave it a purpose in time and in space:
Small as a spark from the fire of creation,
Cradle of life and the home of our race.

Thanks be to God for its bounty and beauty,
Life that sustains us in body and mind:
Plenty for all if we learn how to share it,
Riches undreamed of to fathom and find.

Long have our human wars ruined its harvest;
Long has earth bowed to the terror of force;
Long have we wasted what others have need of,
Poisoned the fountain of life at its source.

Earth is the Lord's: it is ours to enjoy it,
Ours, as his stewards, to farm and defend.
From its pollution, misuse, and destruction,
Good Lord, deliver us, world without end.

Fred Pratt Green

4 This prayer of confession, which was used during worship at an environmental workshop for clergy and lay people:

O God,
your fertile earth is slowly being stripped of its riches,
Open our eyes to see.
O God,
your living waters are slowly being choked with chemicals,
Open our eyes to see.
O God,
your clear air is slowly being filled with pollutants,
Open our eyes to see.
O God,
your creatures are slowly dying and your people are suffering,
Open our eyes to see.
God our maker, so move us by the wonder of your creation,
That we repent and care more deeply.
So move us to grieve the loss of life,
That we learn to cherish and protect your world. [15]

Further liturgical resources on this theme may be found in *New Patterns for Worship*, under the thematic heading 'God in creation', for example, the following confession:

We confess to you
our lack of care for the world you have given us.
Lord, have mercy.
Lord, have mercy.

We confess to you
our selfishness in not sharing the earth's bounty fairly.
Christ, have mercy.
Christ, have mercy.

We confess to you
our failure to protect resources for others.
Lord, have mercy.
Lord, have mercy. [16]

Isaiah's gloomy prophecies

The threefold poetic structure of Isaiah 24.4-6 gives a rolling lugubriousness, a growing sense of doom, like waves crashing on the shore but no longer bound by the sands, coming closer and inexorably closer. Whereas in the first study, 'Living on the edge: the sea', we sensed Wisdom, as spirit and water, flowing through the earth and the people, cleansing, nourishing and purifying sight, now we sense a poison running through the heart of all things. The poison dries up the goodness, and life is sucked away. We are reminded once more of the threat of a crumbling to dust in Job 34.14-15. The curse at the end of Genesis 3 is a dry land: Genesis 3.18a,19b.

The world-upside-down theme is reflected in Proverbs, where the earth is directly affected by the social order: Proverbs 30.21-23. Isaiah continues the theme: Isaiah 3.5.

The scholar Robert Murray points us to another aspect of the world upside down. In the loosened covenant, no one enjoys the fruit of their own labour, whereas under the covenant, the people work and enjoy the fruits of their work: Amos 5.11b, contrast Amos 9.14. [17]

A poem

This powerful poem by a Jewish writer describes the unravelling of the interwoven strands of creation, held together by the cosmic covenant, and torn apart by human greed. It can be used in liturgy or in a study or prayer group to evoke a sense of the threat that human activity can be to creation, and also to the interconnectedness of all creation.

The unmaking of the world

When, in the end, we saw what we had done,
and that we couldn't heal the breach we'd made,
those of us who could
returned to Eden.
None of us were left who feared the fiery, ever-
turning sword.
We'd seen and done and lost too much to care.
Some came as penitents and some with arrogance,
dreaming dreams of New Las Vegas.
When we arrived, the guardians stood waiting at the
gate.
Much to our surprise they let us in; the fiery sword
was sheathed. We failed to see the sadness and the
pity in their eyes.
Some set about to build their castles on the choicest
lakeside spots, but neither earth nor tree would
yield themselves to such. The penitents
knelt humbly, murmuring prayers, asked for little
and were granted less.
When we had all assembled in the breezy time of
day,
we heard the voice of God amidst the trees.
'Where are you?' cried the Voice. 'What have you
done?'
We answered with our tears. No words would do.
'I called you here to witness on this day the thing I
swore I would not do.
I, yes even I, could not foresee what you have done
to one another, to my earth, to my Delight!
I cannot bear to watch the One I love
die such a death. Having made her,
it is only right that I should give to her the gentlest
good night.
Unsaving remnant,
I have called you here to witness the Unmaking of
the World.'
And there was evening, there was morning,
one less day.
We felt the snuffing out of human life, saw family
trees fade out like wisps of smoke as Future carried
with it past into oblivion.
Returned to dust were we,

once blessed as partners of the Lord.
Yet conscious dust were we – no mercy granted here,
and none deserved.
We stood,
mute Golems, left to witness the Unmaking of the
World.
The creeping things, the swarming things, those
that had survived
the worst that we could give,
slipped silently back into mud and dust.
Gone the iridescent wing, the dew-jeweled web.
Gone the peeper's song on summer nights. The
squirrels sat up, alert,
then vanished into mist.
House cat, bobcat, giraffe, coyote, monkey, milk
cow, gone.
And there was evening, there was morning,
one less day.
The birds sang out their warnings, took wing and
disappeared.
Herons stopped their hunting, looked up and
shimmered into fog.
Bright cardinals and tanagers winked out mid-flight
like small red stars.
How loud the silence that they left behind!
We did not see, but felt, the disappearance of the
fish.
Shark and octopus, dolphin, eel and whale abruptly
ended their ballet.
Coral reefs stood empty,
seaweed drifted like torn curtains blowing in the
breeze.
And there was evening, there was morning.
one less day.
As morning came, out faded moon and stars.
And though there was a light, the sun we did not see.
Gone the fiery paintbrush of the dawn,
gone the brilliance at the closing of the day.
No more the silvery gilding of the moon, ended now
the mystery of stars,
and yet
here was evening, there was morning,
one less day.

With the dawning of that day we saw the bleakest
sight of all. No green was left, no living thing at
all. Mighty redwoods fallen back to dirt,
seas of grass turned suddenly to deserts of gray
dust,
no fern, no fruit, no scented breeze, no color to
delight the eye.
The water rose, imperceptibly at first and then
like balm
it covered up the wounded, naked earth.
And there was evening, there was morning,
one less day.
A deluge opened up and rain poured down;
heavens met the earth and
then
there was no earth at all, just wind upon the water
and a silence black and deep.
One last evening, one last morning,
one last day.
God said, 'Let there be darkness.'
And there was –
a darkness deep, unformed and void,
a darkness to eternity for all those called to
witness the Unmaking of the
    World.

Naomi Mara Hyman[18]

SERMON POINTS

- It is becoming less easy to distinguish between
  human and natural disasters, as inappropriate
  stewardship leads to devastating consequences,
  for example, of a tsunami.
- The ancient rituals of atonement and
  reconnection have something we might imitate
  today: formally recognizing harm done to the
  environment and committing to restoration.
- Entering the darkness and absence of Advent is
  a necessary precondition of the coming of the
  light.

Living on the edge 3: Renewal

STUDY NOTES

Dynamic social atoms

In physics, the potential for dynamic and energetic
change is well understood. The world view inherited
from Newton was that the cosmos was constant,
law-abiding and repetitive. Its creator set it up
once and then withdrew. Today, we understand from
quantum mechanics that matter is really bound and
condensed energy. The steam engine turned hard
matter into vibrating energy – something that has
been both very good and very bad for the world.
Trillions of our body's atoms are dissipating every
moment into the world apparently outside, and 98
per cent of them are replaced annually. David Toolan
observes: 'Each of us is a distillation, a condensed
centrifuge of cosmic energy'.[19] Everything in the
universe is internally interconnected through the
fields of atoms. Matter/energy is profoundly social.
The world cannot fall apart. Or, to put it another
way, we stand or fall together.

The uncertainty principle

Moreover, when the particles of energy are not
bound as matter, if you try to locate one, its velocity
will elude you. If you try to measure its speed,
its position will remain unknown. Heisenberg's
Uncertainty Principle, which describes this, makes
Newtonian physics a statistical exercise rather
than a fixed law. In Michael Frayn's brilliant play,
Copenhagen, which is about Heisenberg, the
characters observe:

> [We inherited] the laws of classical mechanics
> ... [They] predate us from the beginning of
> eternity, ... will survive us to eternity's end...
> exist whether we exist or not. Until we come to
> the beginning of the twentieth century, and we're
> suddenly forced to rise from our knees again ...

It starts with Einstein. He shows that measurement – measurement, on which the whole possibility of science depends – measurement is not an impersonal event that occurs with impartial universality. It's a human act, carried out from a specific point of view in time and space, from the one particular viewpoint of a possible observer. Then, here in Copenhagen in those three years in the mid-twenties, we discover that there is no precisely determinable objective universe. That the universe exists only as a series of approximations. Only within the limits determined by our relationship with it.[20]

Later in the play, Heisenberg, a Jew on the run from the Nazis, describes how he eluded death in 1945 by handing a fanatical, exhausted SS soldier a packet of cigarettes, and how the moment hung in the balance – his life, or 20 cigarettes – as one of the soldier's hands starts to open his holster to kill Heisenberg, and the other fingers the packet of Lucky Strike.

God is present throughout the trauma and its resolution

The Hebrew prophets knew that the cosmos was not fixed. God is not a noun, a static entity only to be found in a fixed location, but dynamically present throughout all the movements of creation.

You have heard; now see all this;
and will you not declare it?
From this time forward I make you hear new things,
hidden things that you have not known.
They are created now, not long ago;

before today you have never heard of them,
so that you could not say, 'I already knew them.'
You have never heard, you have never known,
from of old your ear has not been opened.
For I knew that you would deal very treacherously,
and that from birth you were called a rebel.

Isaiah 48.6–9

The Lord's covenant with the cosmos reflects a pattern of destruction and renewal that points again and again to the Lord himself, alone. The reader, humanity, is called to see and understand profoundly what is for ever, what will never end:

Lift up your eyes to the heavens,
and look at the earth beneath;
for the heavens will vanish like smoke,
the earth will wear out like a garment,
and those who live on it will die like gnats;
but my salvation will be for ever,
and my deliverance will never be ended.

Isaiah 51.6

For, says the Lord, ever the lover calling his beloved: 'I am making all things new' (Revelation 21.5).

SERMON POINTS

- Matter is really condensed energy. It is lively and responsive and unpredictable.
- God identifies with matter through the Incarnation.
- God's promise to make all things new will show itself in unexpected and unpredictable ways.

LITURGICAL LINKS

- Worship resources around the theme of renewal may be found within the Pentecost section of *Common Worship: Times and Seasons* (pages 491ff.). The Prayer for Personal Renewal may be adapted for use in this context, as may the Thanksgiving (G80) on page 252 of *New Patterns for Worship*.

- See also the *Additional Collect* for Pentecost:

  Holy Spirit, sent by the Father,
  ignite in us your holy fire;
  strengthen your children with the gift of faith,
  revive your Church with the breath of love,
  and renew the face of the earth,
  through Jesus Christ our Lord.
  Amen.[21]

Christmas

Overarching theme:
How to be a human being who helps the earth rather than harms it.

Practical themes:
- Being a beacon in the community
- Greening your decorations
- Eco-presents
- Recycling
- Switching off

Theological themes:
- The Incarnation models humanity's participation in creation
- Understanding what 'dominion' and 'subduing' might mean
- Understanding what 'tilling' and 'keeping' might mean

Introduction

The coming of the Christ child to the world is the confirmation that, as Word becomes flesh, matter is to be reverenced by Christians. Christ was not a spirit, he was a real, vulnerable, fleshly earthling, a second Adam, identified with *adamah* (the Hebrew word for the land, the 'dust', from which Adam was formed): Genesis 2.7.

The Incarnation is what marks Christianity out from other religions. In Christ, God came to earth in a particular time, space and place, not as a great king in a palace, but as a refugee in a mucky corner borrowed from animals.

It's appropriate, in this context, to think about the role of humanity in relation to the environment, to reconsider the words in Genesis used of the first Adam, and to understand what difference the second Adam, Christ, makes.

Environmental theologians wonder about the words in Genesis that describe humanity's relationship with the rest of the created order: the words 'dominion', 'subdue', 'till' and 'keep'. It's widely understood now that two different authors produced two different creation stories, the first one (Genesis 1 – 2.1a) being a later addition by the priestly editors, known as Deuteronomists. This is not a reason to ignore the story, rather it's a way to understand it better. The priestly story, which uses the words 'dominion' and 'subdue', possibly reflects the hierarchical role the priests had in the society of their time. The words, though, can be understood in a quite gentle sense of keeping the peace (dominion) and cultivating the soil (subdue).

The second, older, account in chapter 2 of Genesis, with its agrarian motifs and its earthy human figure drawn out of the same ground as the creatures, could have been written by a farmer. It is this second Adam who is commanded to 'till' and 'keep' the earth, words that convey a sense of service and preservation. The Second Adam who is Christ, and his Christian disciples, are called to till and keep the earth that has been 'subjected to futility' until now: Romans 8.20.

As Calvin Dewitt has pointed out, *adam* means a human being and *adamah*, the feminine form of the word, means the land (Genesis 2.7).[1] They were, so to speak, a couple. King Uzziah, ruling in a time of plenty, was said to 'love the soil' (2 Chronicles 26.10).[2]

The essence of Christmas is encounter. Encounter means no barriers between us. Theology and ecology teach us that, in fact, there are no barriers, and the flow of life within us is the same life that flows through every creature and through the earth itself, and it is divine.

Practical ideas for Christmas
Colour: white or gold

Being a beacon in the community

Christmas is one of the busiest times of year for most churches. Attendance at Christmas services is on the increase and cathedrals are overflowing. This is a good opportunity, therefore, to show, by being eco-aware in decorations, energy use and in what it chooses to give to others, that the Church cares about the environment.

Christmas traditions

Though we are told he lived in monastic simplicity, Pope Gregory I must have been a good egg, for it was he who urged Augustine of Canterbury to encourage the retention of local customs that were capable of a Christian interpretation. As a result, as Christianity replaced Paganism, Christmas became the name of a high spot of the year.

Mistletoe

Mistletoe, the most pagan of all the symbols of the winter solstice, still finds a place in today's ritual. Some churches banned it, and presumably its traditions, from their premises but York Minster, by contrast, had sprigs of mistletoe carried to the high altar on Christmas Eve. As a parasite, mistletoe can only survive if it has a host. Consequently, with the loss of so many orchards, some has to be imported (it might be worth asking where it has come from when you buy). Mistletoe grows without roots, high above the ground, and often has green leaves when its hosts have none. It was a potion for fertility and an aphrodisiac. Boiled mistletoe was also used to treat epilepsy – a practice that was explained in more recent years when it was found to contain chemicals that have antitumour and sedative properties.

GREENING YOUR DECORATIONS

Christmas decorations provide plenty of opportunities to think green: sprigs of fir, holly, ivy and mistletoe, and the recycling of all sorts of things to bring festive magic, can help show you're green. If you have kept your decorations over the years and feel you would like a change, you can follow a new tradition that has begun in London's Covent Garden, where an empty shop is turned into a decoration exchange. Here you can hand in your old decorations and, having been told their value, can then go to boxes full of decorations given by other people, taking whatever you want to the value of those you have donated.

This could be a great idea for your parish. It would enable everyone to get a new look for their decorations each year without necessitating the production of any new stock, and without expending decoration-miles. The only footprints involved would be those you leave as you walk to and from the parish decoration exchange.

The holly and the ivy

Holly is a must for decoration. England has Europe's oldest holly trees – they are at Stiperstones, Shropshire, and are some 400 years old. Holly is, however, under threat because of climate change. Scientists fear that ozone pollution is causing holly to shed more leaves than usual followed by stunted growth.

Holly is said to represent the crown of thorns, while according to some traditions, the cross itself was made of a holly tree. Each year we sing the carol 'The holly and the ivy', which is full of information about the holly – it bears the crown, its blossom is as white as any flower, its berry as red as any blood, and we hear about the rising of the moon, the running of the deer, the playing of the merry organ and, lest we forget, the sweet singing of the choir, but we learn absolutely nothing about the ivy! There it is in the title and the first line, but in terms of a role, it is on a par with a spare bridegroom at a wedding.

There was a time when **ivy** was banned from some churches, probably because of the custom of ale-stakes (ivy-covered poles that were used to advertise taverns). Ivy has had a bad press, but is a great gift to nature. It is evergreen, its flowers are one of the few plentiful sources of nectar for butterflies and bees in the autumn, and while it may need to be controlled, it does not sap strength from trees when it grows upon them.

But whatever we do to decorate the church, there can only be one thing that really sets the scene.

The Christmas tree

In recent years we have seen a fashion for alternatives to the traditional Christmas tree – an all black tree for the truly trendy households, for instance, and even an upside-down tree to create more space for presents underneath – but the magic and smell of the real tree cannot be beaten.

There is a debate, however, over the eco-merits of imitation and real Christmas trees. On the one hand, man-made trees may last for years, but on the other hand, manufacture is expensive on energy, and during the manufacturing process some trees give off by-products that are harmful to the environment and human health. Moreover, they are then probably transported across the world to be sold. Real trees are carbon neutral because they absorb as much CO_2 when they grow as they release when they decompose or are burned. Many real trees are imported, but sustainable policies are now followed by some British growers.[4]

BAWNING THE THORN

One offspring of the Glastonbury Thorn, a tree now growing at Appleton, has been used to reintroduce bawning or 'adoring' the thorn. This ceremony, which involves decorating the tree with flowers and ribbons, takes place on the third Sunday in June.

Gathering winter fuel

The Christmas tree we know and love is a fairly recent addition to the Christmas tradition, but the burning of the Yule log goes back to ancient times. It was the custom for the members of each household to carry a specially decorated log through the community and light it on Christmas Day to bring light and warmth to the home in the darkest, coldest time of the year. This log would have been cut the previous winter to allow it to season, and ideally it burned from Christmas Day through to Candlemas. If it went out, it was relit at Candlemas and then saved in order to provide kindling for the next Yule celebrations.

The log may have been yew as a hard wood was needed if the log was to stay alight for some weeks. That would be one explanation for the presence of yews in our churchyards. But by all accounts the Yule logs were a fair size and it is questionable whether the yew's slow annual growth could have coped with the demand each year.

An alternative theory points to the fact that the word 'yule' is Scandinavian. Before the coming of Christianity to Scandinavia the Scandinavians had worshipped the ash tree, believing that the first man had been carved from a mighty ash tree, the tree of the world, whose top branches reached up to heaven and whose roots descended into hell. In Britain there were many traditional cures for ailments for which the ash was used and it was said that a sick child passed through the cleft of a tree would be healed. Burning an ash log was said to drive evil spirits from a room.

Holy Thorns

There may be little growing outside the church building at this time of the year, unless you have a cutting of the Holy Thorn of Glastonbury. Legends abound about the hawthorns that have grown at Weary-All Hill to the south of this ancient place in Somerset, all involving the possible visit of **Joseph of Arimathea**, the uncle of Mary. One legend has it that Joseph thrust his staff into the ground, where it took root; another is that the tree grew from a fragment of Christ's crown of thorns. However it came to be there, the tree is very special for it flowers both at Christmas and at Easter. With our current climate in a state of flux, nature must find it difficult to be quite as precise as our legends might wish.

The Puritans destroyed the original tree, but not before cuttings were taken and planted at a variety of sites around the country. A replacement tree was later found for Glastonbury and still today on the second Wednesday in December a piece is cut from it and sent to the Queen.

Eco-presents

As life gets more hectic towards Christmas, we often find there is much last-minute shopping to be done. As a result, everything can become very frenzied and fraught and presents are purchased without enough

PRACTICAL ACTION POINT

Now is a good time to check that water pipes outside the church are lagged.

care and thought about what they are and who they are for – unlike the three gifts brought to the Christ child. More attention and time before buying, or making, could mean less waste. It is estimated that, on average, each person in the UK receives over £35 worth of Christmas gifts that are not really wanted. More than one in ten gifts will languish at the back of drawers and the bottom of wardrobes, equivalent to over £1 billion worth of presents.

Christmas suffers from its share of greenwash, and shops and catalogues have all sorts of products that are designed to appeal to today's eco-aware customers. However, wind-up radios, torches and mobile phone chargers, solar charged appliances, organic clothing and luggage, natural soaps and cosmetics, fair-trade jewellery and chocolate, recycled stationery, potato clocks, organic wine with recycled glasses, are all now produced in a fun, popular and, thankfully, less hair-shirt style.

Switching off

As we said at the start of this section, this is a busy time for the Church, and that goes for the parish or vicar's office. But the point comes when there is simply nothing more that can be done. It is time to shut up shop, go home to the family and have a break. Remember to switch everything off. A computer left on overnight uses enough energy to laser print 800 A4 hymn sheets!

RECYCLE YOUR CARDS

It's not easy to be both green and festive – just look at supermarket shelves and all the packaging and wrapping. Where does it all come from? Where does it all go?

Churches can play their part by offering collection points to encourage the recycling of Christmas cards.

Study notes and sermon points for Christmas

Christmas is the time when God became man and a time when we can think about what it means to be human for God, for ourselves and for our planet.

Being human 1: Humanity as part of the cosmos

STUDY NOTES
In the ecological debate, there is a tendency to see human beings as, at best, irrelevant to the earth's systems. At worst, humanity's capacity for interfering with its environment has meant that other species have suffered from having to adapt to the supremacy of humans or die out. In his book *The Revenge of Gaia*, James Lovelock has characterized the human species as thoughtless adolescents that the earth will have, largely, to destroy as they have become too much of a handful.[5] This is a sorry picture to have at Christmastime, when God himself came to earth as a human being. What is the role of humanity in the cosmos? Is it special in any way?

Humanity as microcosm of the covenant
The cosmic covenant is inclusive of all creatures and could therefore be conceived as according equal value to everything – all are equally of value to God and to one another.

However:
In an evolutionary perspective we have come to see human beings as the embodiment of a line of development that incorporates a number of simpler forms of life. This finds its theological expression in the teaching of St Maximus the Confessor that the human being is the microcosm of creation, the hypostasis of the whole creation community.[6]

Humanity can, then, be seen as the microcosm of the covenant, so that human beings embody within themselves the whole of the created order. In the world of the cosmic covenant, humanity is key both to its destruction and its restoration.

Human behaviour has an effect on the whole cosmos
Isaiah 24's vision of terror indicates that the 'inhabitants' (*yosebim*) have violated the laws and broken the covenant: Isaiah 24.4-6. How do those actions pollute the land? Some hint may be given in the central section of the chapter, in which a chorus shouts in praise of the Lord: Isaiah 24.14-16a. Since all the land is caught up in praise of God, is it the lack of praise that shrivels the land? The effects are severe: the cosmic elements that were bound by oath to keep their allotted roles are shaken to the core: Isaiah 24.18-20.

In the Bible, human wrongdoing harms the earth as much as other people
Robert Murray points out that in Isaiah 24.21b the kings of the earth are the kings of *adamah*.[7] This is the word used in Genesis 2.7 to designate the earth from which Adam was created. The Isaiah passage is the only place in the Hebrew Scriptures where *adamah* is used for the realm of kings, and Murray wonders if, therefore, these kings should be associated with the inhabitants, the *yosebim*, referred to elsewhere in the chapter. If the realm

of activity of the kings is the *adamah*, the soil, then that will be where their wrongdoing, whatever it is, is carried out. A passage in Deuteronomy further underlines this point: Deuteronomy 32.43.

Humanity can also help restore the broken covenant

The earth suffers from the breaking of the covenant; humanity is also punished. But, in some texts, humanity holds within itself the key to restoration. This is shown in the role of the king in the ancient covenant tradition, and in the role of Christ in the New Testament. The royal covenant of Psalm 89 grants David the same power over the waters as the Lord has: Psalm 89.25. In Psalm 72.6, the king is like water falling on mown grass. The king, a human being, has a pivotal role. On him will rest responsibility for justice, and for the fertility of the land.

Christ is the key to restoration and renewal of the earth

There are many references in the New Testament to the Christ as the binding element in creation.[8] Note the bringing together of heaven and earth in Colossians 1.17, 19-20a. In Ephesians 1.8b-10, Paul writes of the Wisdom of God in connection with Christ. In Corinthians and Romans, the theme is the restoration of the whole cosmos: 2 Corinthians 5.17-18a, 19a; Romans 8.19, 21. In Hebrews, Christ is the High Priest and the sacrifice. The ritual of atonement is a key human response to the breaking of the covenant: Hebrews 9.11-12, 15.

So in the biblical understanding of the cosmic covenant, human beings have a role both in its destruction and in its restoration. The cosmic Christ as Wisdom holding all things in creation together is the quintessence of this role. As humanity caught up in that story, we can sing God's praises – Margaret Barker sees this as joining the song of the angels that sustain the forces of creation – atoning for our misuse of creation, and learning how to live rightly with creation.[9]

SERMON POINTS

- Human beings praise God on behalf of all creatures. Everything is nourished by this praise. Withholding praise shrivels up human hearts and the land itself.
- Human behaviour affects everything as everything is bound up in God's cosmic covenant. Not seeing our interconnectedness leads to ill treatment of one another and the land.
- Humanity, through Christ, can restore the broken covenant by seeking to manifest his wisdom in dealing with the earth.

Being human 2: The first creation story

STUDY NOTES

The first account of the creation of the world has a poetic rhythm to it, with its repeated, rolling refrain of God's suffering the creation to come into being, and his repeated perception of its goodness at every stage: Genesis 1.2-4a. It is a well-organized creation that has been wrought: abundant and obedient, hierarchical and unchaotic. The octave of days is complete, and the pinnacle of creation is the seventh day, in which God himself rested (and we don't imagine he did so because he was tired). The passage teaches important lessons of the interrelationship of all creation, from the life-giving oceans and earth to the sustaining green plants for all creatures. Humankind is placed at the top of the created order, twice over given the job of dominion, and ordered by God to subdue the earth. And then given a rest.

This passage is believed to have been written by the priestly class of ancient Israel and added as an introduction to the Hebrew Scriptures. The priests shared the responsibility of government, and were political as well as religious figures of authority. The weight of responsibility for all creatures hangs on the human beings created here.

Image of God

Their being made in the image of God adds potency to the authority of humankind. If this is understood functionally (rather than as a reflection of God's character), the human being becomes the agent of God on earth, the mediator of his presence (like the priests) and is to exercise authority as God's representative.

More subtly, Margaret Barker links this narrative with the parable of the sheep and the goats. Jesus' teaching in Matthew 25 that when you serve one of the least of his brothers and sisters, you serve him, is based on the belief that the human being was made in the image of God.[10]

Dominion

The Hebrew word for dominion is *rada* (Genesis 1.26). Together with the command to subdue (*kabas*, Genesis 1.28), it indicates a 'potent authority', notes Theodore Heibert.[11] What is meant by *rada*? Elsewhere in the Hebrew Scriptures, the word is used in descriptions of military conquest, where it is paired with words such as 'destroy': Numbers 24.19; and 'strike down': Isaiah 14.6.

These are violent images. It is also, however, the word used for the dominion of kings when there was peace on all sides: 1 Kings 4.24; Psalm 72.8. It is used to signify the authority that the head of the house has over servants: Leviticus 25.43, 46, 53; the supervisory role of the king's officials: 1 Kings 5.16; and the rule of their priests: Jeremiah 5.31.

Subdue

The word for subdue is *kabas*, and its uses elsewhere in the Hebrew Scriptures are stronger than *rada*. It implies forcing another into a subordinate position. It is found in the context of military conquest: Numbers 32.22, 29; of a king forcing his people into slavery: Jeremiah 34.11, 16; and of rape: Esther 7.8; Nehemiah 5.5.

Countering this violent usage, Margaret Barker points out that the sense of *kabas* as 'binding' or 'harnessing' could be understood in the creation account as humanity being commanded to do no more than to make the soil productive.[12]

SERMON POINTS

- Being made in the image of God means being mindful of the common good. Humanity has a particular responsibility not to act selfishly.
- In environmental terms, 'keeping the peace' might mean protecting biological diversity, for example, guarding against 'bio-invaders'. In human terms, it might mean protecting social and cultural diversity, ensuring that every unique being has room to flourish.
- 'Subdue' can be re-imagined as making the soil productive.

Being human 3: The second creation story

STUDY NOTES

As we saw in the introduction to this chapter, Genesis 2.4b–25, which is thought to be earlier than the priestly story in Genesis 1, could, by contrast, have been written by a farmer. The different name given to God in this passage, *Yahweh*, has given us the name of the unknown author, the Yahwist. *Yahweh* is a transliteration, formed from the four-letter, unvowelled Hebrew *yod-hei-waw-hei*, which, sounded out with no vowels, is simply a breathing; as the Jewish scholar Arthur Waskow has suggested, one way to translate *Yhwh* is 'Breath of Life'.[13]

Adam and *adamah*

In the story in Genesis 2, creation takes place in arable land, a garden watered by streams. The man is created out of the dust of the earth in the same way as the creatures that follow him. Thus humanity is identified with all growing things, being produced out of the same arable soil. *Adam* is given the role, not of dominating and subduing, but of tilling (*abad*) and keeping or guarding (*shamar*): Genesis 2.15.

Adam is a creature from the earth like all the other creatures. There is no whisper here of domination or subjugation, but rather of service and recognition. *Adamah*, the word for the ground out of which *adam* was formed, is the female form of *adam*: Genesis 2.7. The human and the land are a couple. Prosperity in the time of King Uzziah is described by the Chronicler as characterized by the king's love of the soil: 2 Chronicles 26.10.

Tilling

Elsewhere, the word for tilling, *abad*, is used to express servitude. It is the term that God uses to describe Adam's work after he is expelled from Eden: Genesis 3.23, and is the word used to describe the servitude of one people to another: Exodus 5.9.

These references are resonant of Isaiah's suffering servant in 52.13 – 53.12, and we're thereby reminded of the topsy-turvy kingship of Christ, who was the servant of all and the Lord of all; raised up, but by the cross of suffering and death.

The word *abad* is also used of Israel's worship of God: Exodus 4.23, which is an interesting pointer towards liturgy. The garden of Eden was the model for Moses' tabernacle and the Temple of Solomon that followed it. In the symbolism of the Temple, Adam – humanity – is the high priest. In the garden of Eden, serving and guarding were Adam's liturgy.

Formed from the earth

As though to emphasize the participatory nature of humanity, the same Hebrew phrase – *nepes hayya*, 'formed from the earth' – is used for creatures and human beings – though it has never been translated into the same phrase in English: Genesis 2.7; compare 2.19.

Naming the creatures

Adam's role in naming the animals (Genesis 2.19-20) conveys, by the parallels with the earlier passage (2.7), the sense that he gives them life, as God's breath had given him life. Such an interpretation has its limits – we know that there are millions of species as yet undiscovered by humans and there is no question that their existence is in any way dependent upon that discovery and naming. The contrary would be closer to the truth as the threat of extinction can follow human discovery. Perhaps the passage is teaching its reader that humanity could be content to see and name, and to interfere no more than that.

Naming is a form of respect, of seeing something in its particularity, and it resonates with the ecological perception of the unique diversity of every creature – there are not two blades of grass that are the same. Humanity's participatory, service-oriented role is reflected in the Wisdom tradition within the Hebrew Scriptures, for example, in Psalm 104, where the land and the creatures are fed by the Lord's hand, and in the book of Job.

SERMON POINTS

- In this second creation account, humanity's identity with the earth is emphasized. We feel close to the earth, we love the earth, we are involved with it, we aren't superior to it or detached from it.
- Tilling – *abad* – is Adam's liturgy. The way to handle the creation is to treat it sacramentally, one supreme example being the way we handle the bread and wine in a Communion service.
- Naming creatures can be understood as noticing them. We love what we study.

LITURGICAL LINKS

- A wide range of liturgical resources for Christmas may be found in *Common Worship: Times and Seasons* and its supporting title *Together for a Season* (volume 1). This includes sets of readings for use at carol services.
- A further sequence of readings based around Wisdom Christology forms part of the worshipping tradition at Durham Cathedral and is reproduced by David Kennedy in *Using Common Worship: Times and Seasons – All Saints to Candlemas*, page 88.

Epiphanytide

Overarching theme:
Thinking globally, acting locally

Practical themes:
- Thinking about lights
- Water
- Travel
- Recycling
- Ploughs for today
- Snowdrops
- Renewable power

Theological themes:
- Using the senses to reconnect with the earth's divine source
- Through smell (incense)
- Through taste (water)
- Through sight (light)

Introduction

Epiphanytide runs from the visitation of the Magi to the meeting with Simeon and Anna in the Temple, marked at Candlemas. It is the time when the local event of Christ's birth went global. 'Think global, act local' is a strapline of the environmental movement, coined at the UN Conference on the Human Environment in 1972. Epiphanytide could be a time for Christians likewise to 'think global, act local', for their own very good reasons.

As Epiphany is often portrayed as an explosion of the pinprick of light that came into the world, so we can see how individual behavioural change to lighten our load on the earth, when joined with the changes made by others, becomes an explosion of change in the world. Not only in practical fact – if everyone changed their light bulbs to low energy ones, and switched off all lights and appliances they weren't using, a significant reduction in carbon dioxide emissions would follow – but also in mindset. As more minds turn towards an understanding of the importance of living lightly, so the energy for change grows, until it becomes irresistible, and the leaders of the world have to act.

The president of East Timor spoke of trying to awaken concern and elicit help from the leaders of the world when Indonesian armies crossed his country's borders in the early 1990s. No one would listen – until the BBC sent in the cameras and beamed pictures of the destruction across the world. Then, in his words, 'The mind of the world changed' and he had an appointment with the US president the next day. Help soon followed. The leaders of the democratic world have to do what their electorates want or risk losing their votes. So change starts with individuals coming to understand in their own minds and hearts that the earth matters.

The visit of the Magi signifies the coming of the world to worship Jesus. They are described as wise people from the East bearing gifts of gold, frankincense and myrrh and this links them with the Temple tradition

(see, for example, Exodus 30.1, 6–8) in which frankincense and myrrh were burned on the golden altar of incense. The Temple represents the visible and invisible creation. Wisdom is a gift conferred as one enters the holy of holies, the sanctuary part of the Temple, which represents the invisible world. As such, it symbolizes the perception of that which is beyond space and time, which lies beyond the phenomenal creation, and holds it together in unity. The 'Ah!' moment that we call an epiphany can be perceived in this way. Something is suddenly understood, a light goes on, and we see everything differently. This is the work of Wisdom, which connects everything together, holding the whole of creation in a web of interrelationship: Proverbs 8.22. In the study on Epiphany, we look at the part that incense plays symbolically in Temple liturgy and human transformation, reconnecting us with the creation of which we are a part.

The baptism of Christ takes place in Epiphanytide. Water is an important symbol in Christian teaching, and the Christian and ecological associations with water are discussed in the accompanying study. As David Stancliffe points out, the public ministry of Christ starts with his baptism, in which he submits to the water as a servant, and rises from it anointed by the Holy Spirit.[1] And as each Christian is baptized with the same water and Spirit, so the light is carried out to all the ends of the earth.

Candlemas, with which Epiphanytide ends, is the moment when Jesus is recognized by Simeon in the Temple. The local becomes global again: Jesus' parents are fulfilling the particular, specific ritual requirement of purification, and Simeon recognizes the presence of the light to lighten the whole world. We can link this with the symbolism of the menorah in Solomon's Temple. Representing the tree of life, the menorah is that which offers right perception of the Wisdom underlying the whole creation, by contrast with the tree of knowledge that separates everything out and gives it independent, secular status.

Practical ideas for Epiphanytide: Epiphany

Colour: white

Let your light shine (but not too brightly!)

While Christmas sees the coming together of pagan and Christian traditions, Epiphany brings together the traditions of Eastern and Western forms of Christianity. It is all about **light**. To start with, there is the star – 'leading onward, beaming bright'. No sign of light pollution two thousand years ago and so just imagine how bright that special star had to be to compete with all the stars of the universe. Thank goodness there was no moon!

If your church is floodlit, ensure that all the light is on the building – don't add to the pollution of the heavens!

But the star is only part of the story, for these are busy days. Epiphany involves much coming and going, plus the manifestation of the Trinity at our Lord's baptism and the miracle at Cana. The Greek Church, in its emphasis on the baptism of Christ, has chosen 'the day of lights' on which to celebrate the baptism because of the enlightenment it produces.

Epiphanytide gives us further opportunity to consider lighting and its effects, costs and conservation. This could be just the time to be **auditing your lighting**, its source and its use throughout the church buildings and to let everyone know within and without the church community that this is what you are doing. The audit can be carried out whenever you wish, at different times by different people. The start of a new year, however, is a good time both to stop smoking and to do an environmental audit to identify the changes that could be managed throughout the coming year.

In *Times and Seasons*, it is suggested that the new year is an opportunity to renew our covenant with God, acknowledging how we have failed in the past:

> *For the sin that has led us to misuse your gifts,*
> *evade our responsibilities,*
> *and fail to be good stewards of your creation:*
> *Lord have mercy.*
> **Lord forgive.**[2]

SPONSORING THE LIGHTS

Some churches, such as Avening parish church in Gloucester, are saving energy by limiting their floodlighting to special occasions, with members of the congregation and local community invited to 'sponsor' an evening's illumination to commemorate the death of a loved one, or to celebrate a wedding and other significant events.

These are short days and so there is need for light – use it to highlight special features within the church, but don't waste it!

The sound of many waters

The Eastern Church remembers Christ's baptism and its use of **water** by blessing the waters and giving thanks for them as the source of life. In Russia it has been the custom to cut a cross in the frozen waters of rivers and lakes and for the priests to dive into the water below. With the recent milder winters, however, there has been no ice – the climate taking its toll on another tradition.

Water is a key theme of the season of Epiphany – water into wine, the waters of the River Jordan, the waters of creation, the water of baptism, the Jerusalem Temple's Water Gate, the call beside the Sea of Galilee.

The limits that God sets on the force and movement of the waters are immeasurable, but all too often we take them for granted. There is no such thing as new water.

All that was created is all we have and will ever have, but as each year passes, greater demands are placed on this precious resource. Water is so fundamental to life that it controls most of the world's local, regional and national boundaries. It is a force to be reckoned with: it has its own power, as anyone who has attempted DIY plumbing will know only too well.

At the turn of a tap?

The slogan 'think global, act local' could not be more appropriate than at Epiphanytide, with its emphasis on water. If our local water supply stops or is rationed, we are greatly inconvenienced; thankfully, it is usually always there at the turn of a tap. While we try to conserve our own supplies in a variety of ways, we can help and pray for others who are working to bring water to the many places around the world where there is little or no water, or it is unfit to drink.

There are many projects run by a variety of organizations, who always need support. Here is another opportunity to help projects in twinned parishes or dioceses. If there are no appropriate .

A TIME TO RECYCLE

With Twelfth Night comes the task of taking down the decorations and deciding what to do with the Christmas tree. Some trees will go back into the vestry cupboard, while others may have roots and simply return to a quiet and normal life until next year. But trees just bought for the occasion should be recycled (see page 26).

Some churches turn their Christmas tree into a cross to use the following Eastertide (see Recycling the Christmas tree: the Lenten cross, page 56).

schemes through these links, then contact organizations such as Tearfund (see Appendix 2: Useful contacts).

Tearfund are helping to overcome drought in the Niger where climate change has upset rainfall patterns. Help is being given to communities to dig wells and build dykes so that when the rains do come the water can be controlled and managed in order to irrigate the land and grow wild wheat.

Back to work!

All good things must come to an end, as medieval merrymakers well knew. Plough Monday was the first day back to work: a real start to a new year. The day prior to Plough Monday – **Plough Sunday**, the first Sunday of Epiphany – is still celebrated by some churches, who use it as an opportunity to ask a blessing on human labour near the start of the calendar year:

> By your blessing, let this plough be a sign of all that you promise to us. Prosper the work of our hands, and provide abundant crops for your people to share.[3]

PLOUGHS FOR TODAY

Few of us today will have access to a plough, but there may be other implements in daily use that have a similar 'initiating' role in tasks and enterprises that are undertaken today. Environments and projects differ and so your congregation may choose a very different 'plough' from that of a neighbouring parish.

UNWANTED PLOUGHS

Plough Sunday could be an opportunity to collect unwanted tools that would find willing users elsewhere in the world. Tools for Self Reliance is a national organization that collects and refurbishes tools of all kinds to send to rural communities in Africa. Not all tools are needed, so do look at www.tfsr.com before organizing a collection. Blacksmiths', carpentry and engineering tools are always needed. So, too, are tools for the repair of bicycles, shoes, automobiles and electrical equipment.

Tools for Self Reliance do not need gardening tools, but these are collected by The Conservation Foundation's Tools Shed project, which aims to take tools out of the waste stream and recycle them for use in schools and community projects. The refurbishing is currently being done by inmates of Wandsworth Prison and it is hoped that the scheme may be extended to other prisons around the country.

LITURGICAL LINKS

- *Common Worship: Times and Seasons* provides a range of liturgical resources for the season of Epiphany, including a service for the Festival of the Baptism of Christ (page 184).
- Traditional resources for Plough Sunday can be found in *Common Worship: Times and Seasons* (page 607).

Practical ideas for Epiphanytide: Candlemas

Candlemas, which entered the Christian calendar in the sixth century, celebrates the purification of Mary and the presentation of Jesus at the Temple in Jerusalem. Jesus was met by Anna and Simeon and the Gospel of Luke records that Simeon held the baby Jesus and called him the light of the world.

> *He searches the hearts of all your people*
> *and brings to light the image of your splendour.*
> *Your servant Simeon acclaimed him as the light of*
> *the world*
> *while Anna spoke of him to all who looked for all*
> *your redemption.*[4]

Hence the custom of celebrating light on this day by blessing all the candles to be used in the church throughout the year. Candlemas is celebrated on 2 February, the fortieth day after the nativity, midway between the shortest day of the year (21 December) and the spring equinox.

At this time of the year, the Celts celebrated the festival of the goddess Brigit as a rite of purification and fertility, which became the Christian festival of St Bride, often held on Candlemas.

Candlemas bells

Nature's signs of the time are the flowers known as Candlemas bells, also called Mary's taper, a reference to the ancient Christian tradition of distributing tapers for worship on this day. They are better known now as **snowdrops**. We sometimes come across these signs of early spring in wild places, as if these were their natural habitats, but who knows who may have planted them to look that way, for snowdrops are not recorded as growing wild until the late 1700s. Before that they were limited to gardens, especially in monasteries. Indeed, snowdrops, which look almost nun-like and at prayer, have had a special place in Catholic churches as a symbol of Candlemas and purity. In non-Catholic households, by contrast, the snowdrop, like some other white flowers and blossom, is considered an unlucky guest.

Today, both Anglican and Catholic churches hold Snowdrop Sunday services to remember the victims of cancer and pray for those involved in the care of cancer patients, and in cancer research. Some churches, such as St Mary's, Kirkbramwith, Doncaster, have a Snowdrop festival.

 In 1998, the Wiltshire Living Churchyard Project began to manage the churchyard of St Giles' Church in the village of Stanton St Quintin. Thanks to the efforts of enthusiastic volunteers, the churchyard is now a wildlife haven with over one hundred flower and grass species recorded.[5]

ALTERNATIVE POWER

Power from the ground

St Mary's Church, Welwyn, Hertfordshire, recently installed a Ground Source Heat Pump (GSHP), which takes heat out of the ground under the churchyard and then pumps it around the church buildings. The installation involves 18 boreholes, which go down about 30 metres to bring up the heat. There are no fumes, and there is no smell, no noise and no carbon dioxide – unlike the alternative gas boiler, which would have emitted 44 tonnes of carbon dioxide annually. The GSHP, which cost £40,000, is reported to be working well and reducing its annual carbon footprint to one and a half tonnes. Roger Carden, fund-raiser for the project, says, 'It is certainly not an investment in the financial sense – it would be better to put the money in a building society than spend it this way – that is, if you don't care about the environment.'[6]

Power from the wind

The church at Stocks-in-Bowland, Lancashire, is so remote that wind power was the only affordable choice of electricity. Wind power was a third of the cost of solar power. Although the church is in an area of natural beauty, permission was granted to build a turbine, which now generates power that is then stored in batteries to produce all the power needed for heating, lighting and time locks.

Power from the sun

Two London churches have installed solar panels. St Aldhelm's, close to the North Circular Road, has 108 solar panels on the south-facing roofs of its church hall. The installation cost almost £90,000 and, although grants were received, the church had to raise £13,500 from its own resources. It hopes, however, that reduced fuel bills will enable this amount to be saved within six years. The vicar, David Bolster, says, 'This is only the beginning. We do not see ourselves as pioneers, only as Christians doing what we can with the opportunities and resources we have. However, we may well be a beacon.'

The second church is one that many thousands of visitors to London will know as it is only a few yards from Piccadilly Circus. Often the heritage authorities refuse permission to install solar panels on church buildings, but the congregation at St James', Piccadilly, which was designed by Sir Christopher Wren and is a grade 1 listed building, found that it was possible to install a PV system on the flat, south-facing roof over the south aisle where it is invisible from street level and does not need roof-piercing fixings. After 16 months of installation, the system generated about 5000 KWh of electricity and saved about eight tonnes of carbon dioxide.

Many churches are looking at solar panels as a way of using God's light to provide power for the church and income by selling surplus energy. However, Simon Dawson, who was part of the working group that was instrumental in developing the project, advises other churches to consider solar power only if it is part of an overall footprint-reduction project based on a sound environmental audit and is not a stand-alone project. Energy usage reduction projects may be more cost effective.[7]

Alternative power is of interest to many churches – the Shrinking the Footprint audit (see page 00) has found several that are still unconnected to any form of energy source and where candle power still reigns!

A Sabbath for the land

Candlemas also marks the start of the setting aside of Lammas-land so that the grasses in areas of grazing can be allowed to grow undisturbed until midsummer. (Lammas-land was hay meadows that were kept free of any agricultural practice to allow grass and flowers to grow naturally from Candlemas (2 February) until midsummer. Later on Old Lammas Day (13 August) the meadow would be closed again until late September, early October for the grass to grow for winter grazing. The then Nature Conservancy Council published figures showing that we had lost 95 per cent of our flower-rich meadows – and that was in 1984. Bring back Lammastide!) Like us, like God on the seventh day, the land needs to rest. Not long ago it was the practice to move crops from field to field, and allow some land to lie fallow. This was a time for the soil to breathe and be restored. But the industrialization of agriculture and the use of chemicals has meant the exclusion of simple rules that gave the earth opportunities to rest and recover in order to serve well again.

We now have land little better than desert because we think we cannot afford to wait a while and let nature live without our continuous involvement. Our country churchyards are often oases of biodiversity surrounded by chemically controlled mono-culture. Some may complain that these churchyards look untidy and uncared for, but perhaps we can campaign for at least part of the churchyard to be allowed to grow wild. It could have a beauty and biodiversity that is unique. If all our churchyards could be havens of wildlife, they would add up to a huge national park supporting an unparalleled store of biodiversity.

God-given power

During a season involving the celebration of light, it is fitting to consider how we might utilize the light and heat that comes naturally. After all, many churches have south-facing roofs, which should be natural homes for modern technological innovation. But the cells, panels or pipes that need to be installed come at a cost, either to the churches, or to the power companies, which provide grants.

It is possible to produce plenty of hot water in this country, and though hot water is not always a major need for churches, those providing facilities for the homeless do find that, once they have installed a hot water heating panel, the virtually free hot water is a boon. Most churches, however, are more interested in electricity production, especially if they can produce more than they need on Sundays and the rest of the week can sell electricity to the National Grid. Examples are thin on the ground but will no doubt increase as the costs go down.

During Epiphany we can take the opportunity to use our senses of smell, taste and sight to reconnect with the creation.

Study notes and sermon points for Epiphanytide

Smell, taste and sight 1: Epiphany and incense

STUDY NOTES

Incense and the Temple, indicating the everlasting presence of God

The visitors from the East brought gifts of gold, frankincense and myrrh. Incense is traditionally associated with the gaining of Wisdom. In our ecological context, Wisdom makes it possible to reconnect with creation so that humanity will treat the earth properly.

In Exodus 30.1, 6-8, the commandment to keep the incense burning perpetually is an indicator of the cosmic covenant, the berit 'olam, God's everlasting presence. The cloud of incense meant that the Lord was present: Leviticus 16.2. The incense, among other Temple goods, was 'most holy', which meant that its holiness was infectious — you caught it by touching it: Exodus 30.29. References to 'cloud', 'pillar of fire', 'fire', 'coals', are all reminiscent of Temple incense.

Incense and purification

In other passages, a vision of God invokes judgement. We can understand judgement to mean purification. We are purified of our mistaken thinking of ourselves as lords of creation. Materialistic greed prevents right seeing and cuts us off from Wisdom.
Isaiah has a vision of God in the smoke of the incense, and sees his own uncleanness by virtue of that light: Isaiah 6.1-5. The seraphim then effect a cleansing by means of coals from the altar of incense, leading to Isaiah's offering himself as a messenger. He has become clean and empty, and knows he is an expression of the divine oneness of God: Isaiah 6.6-8. The message he is given is paradoxical, or is it a macrocosm of what Isaiah himself has faced: Isaiah 6.9-13? Until the complete purification of the land and the people, there will be no Wisdom. An account in Ezekiel describes the coals from the altar of incense being used to purge the city: Ezekiel 10.2. Vision, purification and judgement appear together in the book of Revelation: Revelation 1.7; 8.3-5, 8-9; 10.1.

Incense and Wisdom

As a passage in Ecclesiasticus shows, Wisdom literally smells sweet:

> Like cassia and camel's thorn I gave forth perfume, and like choice myrrh I spread my fragrance, like galbanum, onycha, and stacte, and like the odour of incense in the tent.
>
> Ecclesiasticus 24.15

Other passages associate the fragrance of incense with Wisdom. In the famous messianic passage from Isaiah 11.2-3, the word often translated 'delight' ('quick understanding' in the Authorized Version) is 'fragrance' in Hebrew. The Messiah's fragrance was in the fear of the Lord, and as Proverbs tells us, the fear of the Lord is the beginning of Wisdom: Proverbs 1.7. The fragrance of God is referred to in 2 Corinthians 2.14-15. It is a long-standing tradition within Christianity that the saints smell sweet, even after their bodies have died.

The fragrance of Christ's teaching

The early Christians became the embodiment of the Wisdom of God, diffusing the divine sweetness and knowledge of God. Notice that in 2 Corinthians 2.14-17, knowledge is absolutely appropriate to the hearer: for some it is life, while for others it is death. It is an invitation to those who see it as such but the fragrance of decay to those caught in the myth of separation from God. The invitation from Wisdom is to understand what we are in truth – this is the purification through the burning coals of incense. Sin (literally, 'missing the mark') is dissolved as the self we thought we were is dissolved, the self that is a shell made of a collection of identities, belongings, beliefs and attachments.

According to the *Apocalypse of Moses*, when Adam was thrown out of Paradise, he took herbs and spices from the Garden for incense.[8] This emphasizes the linking of the Temple and Eden, with the incense a sweet reminder of the garden of Eden.

SERMON POINTS

- Incense is associated with the presence of God; it conferred holiness; in its clouds people had visions of God and experienced purification; its lingering fragrance embodied Wisdom; and it evoked memories of Paradise.

- Judgement and purification bring about the possibility of seeing creation aright.
- The seeds of Paradise, the sweet-smelling incense, so evocative of memory, remind us of what we have apparently lost. The incense is our invitation to remember again who we truly are, to realize that this soil against which we labour is created by the same one God as our own body/minds are, and is a glorious celebration of its source.

Smell, taste and sight 2: The baptism of Jesus and water

STUDY NOTES

The significance of water

The baptism of Jesus takes place at Epiphanytide. Water nourishes all creatures, and binds the dusty particles of earth into clods. It ensures fertility. Its withdrawal bodes disaster and so does its inundation. As God creates and recreates the covenant, he signifies his act by letting the waters flow: Job 38.25-27. No human being had a hand in this fertilization of the land, nor was it done for the sake of any human inhabitant. This indicates that the covenant is for the sake of all creation, not just humanity.

LITURGICAL LINK

Common Worship: Times and Seasons includes the following prayer for use at the offering of incense:

> *Blessed are you, Lord our God, King of the universe:*
> *to you be praise and glory for ever!*
> *As our prayer rises up in your presence as incense,*
> *so may we be presented before you*
> *with penitent hearts and uplifted hands*
> *to offer ourselves in your priestly service.*
> ***Blessed be God for ever!***[9]

In Isaiah, by contrast, it is the human element, the restoration of social justice through the kings of Israel, that is like water flowing in a parched land: Isaiah 32.1-3. The soil, the animals and the people are all the beneficiaries of the reopening of the heavens: Psalm 78.15-16; Joel 2.21-24. These are powerful images to set against scenes of lands parched by lack of water due to climate change; or flooded land where the water has become poisonous.

Water gives life

The Temple was seen as the source of life-giving water, both in the sense of food and in the sense of healing: Ezekiel 47.1, 2b, 8-9,12. This vision is repeated in Revelation: Revelation 22.1-2. In Isaiah the knowledge of God is compared to water, penetrating to the heart of all things and flowing on: Isaiah 11.9b.

Water restores fertility and vision

The Spirit, here depicted as flowing like water, is directly associated with the restoration of fertility: Isaiah 32.15. The pouring out of the water in the wilderness is connected in the passage below with the restoration of sight. In the world view of the cosmic covenant, blindness is the ignorance or abuse of knowledge that is learned from the fallen angels, a state of bondage to evil: Isaiah 35.5-7a.[10] This passage is reminiscent of the one from Isaiah read by Jesus in Luke 4.18 (compare Isaiah 61.1ff.). The Isaiah passage continues: 'I will make an everlasting covenant with them . . .' (Isaiah 61.8c).

In the story of the man born blind receiving his sight, Jesus spits on to earth and makes mud, and it is this water in the earth that restores the man's sight. The man, now able to see, knows that what has happened comes from God: John 9. The vision of God (in this case by meeting and recognizing the Christ) brings the gift of true sight, of true Wisdom. The restoring forces of Wisdom and water are connected, and we gain a sense of a cosmos flowing with life, which is joined in all parts to itself by living water: Job 38.36-38. In the New Testament, John's Jesus tells Nicodemus: 'Very truly, I tell you, no one can enter the kingdom of God without being born of water and Spirit . . . You must be born from above' (John 3.5,7; see also 4.10,14).

Baptism as a gateway to the divine

In the outer temple of Solomon's day there was a bronze basin. It was huge, half the width of the Temple courtyard, and was known as 'the sea'. In the Temple tradition, the Temple was thought of as surrounded by the sea: Ezekiel 47.1ff.[11] The Temple sits over the waters, keeping them in check by virtue of God's presence on his throne in the holy of holies: Psalm 93. The sea acts like the veil of the Temple, guarding the holy of holies.

Margaret Barker points us to the *Clementine Recognitions*, an early Christian text attributed to Clement of Rome (c. AD 100), in which God separated the once-joined heaven and earth with ice. This is the 'sea of glass' of John's vision in Revelation 15.2, and Ezekiel also saw it: Ezekiel 1.22. 'Crystal' here means, literally, 'terrible ice'. In this passage in Ezekiel, the connection is made between the role of the cherubim and the sea both in protecting the sanctuary and in being a way into it: Ezekiel 1.23-26. With baptism, the water stops being a barrier and becomes a gateway to the divine.

The tradition that Eden was surrounded by sea[12] is reflected in Revelation 4.6; 15.2. The sea is to be crossed to reach the holy of holies. This is perhaps the meaning of the miracles of Christ as he walked on the water or calmed the storms.

LITURGICAL LINK

You may wish to use the Prayer over the water at Holy Baptism (Epiphany) from *Common Worship: Christian Initiation*, page 153.

A poem

I built my house by the sea

I built my house by the sea.
Not on the sands mind you
Not on the shifting sand.
And I built it of rock.
A strong house
By a strong sea.
And we got well acquainted, the sea and I.
Good neighbours,
Not that we spoke much.
We met in silences,
Respectful, keeping our distance
But looking our thoughts across the fence of sand.
Always the fence of sand our barrier,
Always the sand between.
And then one day
(and I still don't know how it happened)
The sea came.
Without warning.
Without welcome even.
Not sudden and swift, but a shifting across the
sand like wine
Less like the flow of water than the flow of blood,
Slow but flowing, like an open wound.
And I thought of flight, and I thought of drowning,
and I thought of death.
But while I thought the sea crept higher till it
reached my door.
And I knew that there was neither flight nor death
nor drowning.
That when the sea comes calling you stop being
good neighbours,
Well acquainted, friendly from a distance
neighbours.
And you give your house for a coral castle
And you learn to breathe under water.

C. Bialock[13]

SERMON POINTS

- Water can bring life and it can destroy. Drought kills and so does flooding.
- The water from Christ brings true vision and rebirth.
- In baptism the water that guards the divine stops being a barrier and becomes a gateway.

Smell, taste and sight 3: Candlemas and the menorah

STUDY NOTES

Candlemas celebrates the meeting of Simeon and Anna with the Christ child when he is brought to the Temple for the first time. Simeon recognizes the true High Priest and declares that he will be a 'light to lighten the Gentiles'. Candlemas is a celebration of light moving out from the local to the global. Encountering the light lightens the world everywhere we look, changes our relationship with it, and changes the way we behave towards it.

Light in the Temple

The liturgical light in Moses' tabernacle and Solomon's Temple was the menorah or seven-headed candlestick. It is described in Exodus 25.31–40; 37.17–24. The first description mentions the vision of Moses on Mount Sinai when, as well as the Ten Commandments, he was shown a vision of the underlying patterns of creation, see for example, Exodus 25.40. It was the pattern and order of this creation that Moses mimicked in the fashioning of his tabernacle, a pattern that Solomon followed when he built his Temple. The menorah, in the tabernacle and Temple, stood for the lights in the firmament: the sun, moon and the five planets known to the ancient world.

The menorah as the eyes of God

In fact, the menorah has many layers of meaning. One is that it is God's eyes, symbolized by the almond-shaped cups: Zechariah 4.10b. Jeremiah sees the almond branch and understands that this symbolizes the Lord's watchfulness: Jeremiah 1.11-12. The Hebrew word for almond (*shaqed*) is very like the word for watching (*shoqed*). The eyes of God are distilled throughout the phenomenal creation. Their being likened to almonds gives them a sensual reality; they are not some spooky ethereal not-thing, but right there, looking back at us through the forms of creation. The presence of God throughout creation is here given a consciousness: the presence of God is understood as a witnessing presence. Just as our body/minds see, so all things see, but it is really the oneness of God seeing, through all things. Martin Buber wrote:

> It is part of our concept of a plant that it cannot react to our action towards it: it cannot 'respond'. Yet this does not mean that here we are given simply no reciprocity at all ... That living wholeness and unity of the tree, which denies itself to the sharpest glance of the mere investigator and discloses itself to the glance of one who says Thou, is there when he, the sayer of Thou, is there: it is he who vouchsafes to the tree that it manifests this unity and wholeness; and now the tree which is in being manifests them.[14]

Menorah as the tree of life

The almond shapes are reminiscent of Aaron's rod, which came to life when placed in the holy of holies of the Temple: Numbers 17.8. Wisdom is described as the tree of life in Proverbs 3.18, but the clearest link between the menorah and the tree of life is in Enoch, who describes it as fiery: 'gold looking and crimson, with the form of fire' (2 Enoch 8.4).

Light and messiahship

If 'light' and 'branch' signify menorah, then it was associated with kingship: 2 Samuel 21.17; 1 Kings 11.36; 2 Kings 8.19, and it becomes a messianic title as it is associated with David: Isaiah 4.2; 11.1; Jeremiah 23.5; 33.15; Zechariah 3.8; 6.12-13. The Hebrew word for the branches of the lamp is *qanim*, meaning reed. Isaiah picks up this imagery in Isaiah 42.3-4. Revelation speaks of the one like the Son of Man among the lampstands: Revelation 1.12-16. There follows the explanation that the stars are the angels and the lampstands the churches, as we saw above: Revelation 1.20. Christ is the light, and the churches and their leaders are the conveyers of that light, but not separable from it, just as sunbeams are not separable from the sun. You may wish to look up a poem by Mary Oliver entitled 'The Sun' (in her *New and Selected Poems*, Beacon Press, 1992).

SERMON POINTS

- The local experience in our own hearts of the light of Christ goes global at Candlemas; in relation to the environment we are enjoined to think globally but act locally.
- Light, symbolized in the menorah as the eyes of God, can be experienced as the creation 'looking back at us' if we see it with eyes of Wisdom.
- The Church is also the light of Christ gone global, like the rays of the sun.

LITURGICAL LINKS

There are numerous liturgical resources on the theme of light in *Common Worship: Times and Seasons* (see the Advent, Christmas and Epiphany sections) and in the supporting book *Together for a season: Advent, Christmas and Epiphany*.

Lent

Overarching theme:
Repenting of greed and undertaking to live simply

Practical themes:
- Labyrinths
- Enough is enough
- Mothering Sunday
- Flower concern
- The Lenten Cross

Theological themes:
- Rethinking dominion
- Choosing the tree of wisdom not the tree of knowledge
- Removing the veil of misperception

Introduction

Lent begins with Ash Wednesday, the day on which we enrol for the time of withdrawal, penitence, reflection and discipline that is the Lenten period.

Ash Wednesday is when we are reminded that we came from dust and to dust we will return. The phrase is from the dark rebukes of God on Adam's expulsion from Paradise, but this same dust is the *adamah*, the ground from which Adam sprang, the feminine form of *adam*, the land that is his lover. Ash Wednesday, then, is a time to remember our creatureliness, with due humility, and with the positive sense of participation in the created order as part of the cosmic web of interdependence. We are bound to one another and to God in this web and we cannot do without one another and the rest of creation. Even hermits share the atmosphere, the water cycle and the ground we all walk on.

In the second creation story, Genesis 2.4b-25, Adam and Eve ate from the tree of knowledge and this was the disobedience that led to their expulsion. One way of telling this story that helps our environmental understanding is to say that Adam and Eve chose fruit from the wrong tree.

There are two ways of seeing, symbolized by the two trees in Paradise. One is the tree of knowledge, which separates us from one another, the land, and our divine creator. We see things as hermetically sealed individuals, independent and unsustaining because we have been disconnected from our source. This is the tree that Adam and Eve chose to eat from. The other tree, the tree of life, from which they were not initially debarred, offers Wisdom. Wisdom is aware of the unity underlying all things, is aware of the lively Spirit sustaining all things, and wise seeing has no separation in it: '[Wisdom] is a tree of life to those who lay hold of her' (Proverbs 3.18).

Richard Chartres has said, ominously:

The pursuit of fragmented knowledge, divorced from any consciousness of ourselves as creatures, fashions a knower who looks out on the world about him and sees, not an animate nature in which he is a participant, but simply matter to be exploited. Choosing the wrong tree progressively degrades a human being into someone who gets used to the dull pain of seeing nature as a lifeless desert and of treating its beauty as a deceptive mask. Dominance is substituted for connectedness in this way of knowing the universe . . .

The habit of regarding everything as an object has even infected our good opinion of ourselves. Beneath much of the rhetoric about human dignity lurks a reductionist suspicion that we are little more than upright animals, or even just rapacious bipeds whose happiness lies in consuming the world and treating other people as commodities to be used for our pleasure.[1]

Lent is a time of transformation – not the sudden epiphanic 'Ah!' of realization, but a slow, unfolding, reflective, careful time in which we prune ourselves for better growth, restraining desires and stilling urges, giving time to God for his transforming power to work in us. It is a Sabbath time. It is not to be thought of as an exhausted rest after a year of consumption, drawing breath before carrying on consuming. Nor is it, as it so often can become, an excuse for detoxification. It's a time to express penitence. It is also a time to take rest seriously, to realize the limitations on the physical universe, to be quiet, to contemplate without rushing into action. It is a time of seeds growing secretly in the dark, nothing showing, nothing known, nothing assumed or predicted. It is a journey through the wilderness, a time to feel the pain of the world without knowing that anything can be done about it, feeling the pain and not turning away from it, accompanying the pain as a friend and lover, helpless for a time, but always faithful. It is an unresolved, haunting melody.

Practical ideas for Lent

Seasonal colour: purple/blue/the 'natural' unbleached linen of Lenten array

Lent begins in a garden that is well tended and beautiful, but as the story unfolds we learn about choice and its consequences, which provides us with an opportunity to reflect on everything we use and what we waste.

If this is a time when individuals within the Church are doing without, maybe a darkened church would send a message to the rest of the community. Lent could be an opportunity, therefore, for the church to show that this is time of reflection by **switching off all the floodlighting**.

Labyrinths

Some churches create labyrinths at this time. Labyrinths go back to 2000 BC and those of us who have had the chance to experience them know how they can clear the mind and allow thought and meditation to gain strength within us.

There are those who take Lent to mean every day except Sundays. If Sundays do not count, then Lent ends at Easter. However, if you include Sundays within Lent, then the 40 days end on Palm Sunday with Jesus entering Jerusalem. This provides a link to Lenten labyrinths, for the centre of the labyrinths at Chartres and the other great cathedrals is known as 'Jerusalem'. Thus those who made a pilgrimage through the labyrinths, often on their knees, were on their way to Jerusalem, and a journey through a labyrinth during Lent had a very special meaning – and it still has, even today.

Internal environment audit

Lent is not just an opportunity to confess, having eaten up everything on Shrove Tuesday that we cannot eat for the next few weeks, it's also an opportunity to carry out a complete **internal environmental audit** of our very being and to set targets, which begin on Ash Wednesday. For then we live without for 40 days.

In a wilderness it would certainly be simpler. In our material world, in which everything is designed to

LENT LABYRINTH

Originally created in lights on New Year's Eve to celebrate the new millennium, the labyrinth in the cloisters of Norwich Cathedral has become a permanent feature and is now used for a Lent pilgrimage. The labyrinth was created by Jane Sunderland, who walks the labyrinth every day in Lent, and holds workshops in the refectory, based on her book, *Walking the Labyrinth*, in which she gives history, reflection and meditation.[2]

See also the Grove booklet *Labyrinths and Prayer Stations*.[3]

FLOWER CONCERN

The UK is one of the biggest importers of flowers in the world. Over half come from Holland where many are treated with fertilizers and pesticides and forced to flower out of season in huge, heated greenhouse factories. Many others come from Kenya – a vital income for this poor country – but involving considerable flying miles and carbon dioxide emissions. Our Government encourages us to buy from Africa, explaining that flowers grown there use less energy because they are not grown in heated greenhouses. However, there is another cost – many workers in Columbia and Kenya earn less than half a living wage and toxic chemicals are often used with little control.

There are now fair-trade certified flower farms in Kenya. UK-grown, organic and fair-trade suppliers, are listed in ***www.flowers.org.uk*** while ***www.fairflowersfairplants.com*** gives FTP certified British retailers.

As an alternative, can you grow your own flowers to reflect local provenance and the seasons?

Following the traditions of many clergy, the Rt Revd Tony Foottit has published a delightful book, *A Gospel of Wild Flowers*, in which he describes the wonders of wild flowers and their spiritual significance and power to nourish the soul.[4]

make us consume, we cannot pretend that it's easy to go without. Manufacturers seem to be for ever bringing out new models of everything that we have, and then on our side, a combination of fashion, greed and craving makes these 'must haves'. Lent is in early spring so it is a good time for a mental **spring clean** of what we have and need.

Enough is enough

Lent is not just living without, it's a chance to experience a lifestyle of enoughness, showing us just what we *could* live without. It's our personal 40-day sustainable development training course and endurance test rolled into one.

It's also a good time to think of people elsewhere in the world who do not enjoy enough – enough food, enough water, enough of the basic necessities of life. Lent might be a good time to find out about the impact of environmental change on some of the world's poorest communities – Tearfund and Christian Aid have produced resources to help here (see Appendix 2: Useful contacts) – and to think about what you as a

church can do to help.

Mothering Sunday

Mid-Lent Sunday is also Mothering Sunday, and a great opportunity to bring flowers into the church at a time when they are not normally present. While it's a nice idea to think of our mothers on this day, the tradition originates not from a family service in the local church, but from a service for young people in their mother church or nearest cathedral. This was the one day in the year when young people in service were given a day off. Having attended their mother church, they would walk home – is this a tradition you could encourage today? – through lanes filling with spring flowers. The young people would pick bunches

The flora of the parish of St Andrew, Kenn, Devon, has been recorded in a booklet by Tony Walshe.[5] The booklet records the origins and ecology of this rural site, which dates to medieval times.

of flowers and take them home to their mothers – hence our custom of giving flowers on this day.

While it's good to give flowers, it does raise a number of environmental and social issues – not least questions about where the flowers in our churches come from and under what circumstances they are grown and harvested. **This might be a good time to review the sourcing of your church's flowers.**

Church gardens

The garden featuring in the worship at this time might inspire the **development or restoration of an actual garden within the church site**. While many churches have space, many do not and so here is an opportunity for creative thinking. Even the straggly flowerbeds around your modern church building could be made more beautiful.

St Valentine's Day is the traditional time for sowing onions and garlic seeds.

RECYCLING THE CHRISTMAS TREE: THE LENTEN CROSS

As the time of Easter nears, the Christmas tree, which has been stored safely since Twelfth Night, can be stripped of its branches to prepare it for its service as a **Lenten Cross**. *Together for a Season* includes a 'Lenten tree pathway', which is an excellent guide to planning a variety of practical ways to develop worship throughout Lent.[6] It includes full instructions on preparing your Lenten cross.

Study notes and sermon points for Lent

Lent is a time to withdraw and take stock. Penitence for the ways we have misused God's planet and renunciation of our acquisitive natures can be practised during this time.

Penitence and renunciation 1: Inappropriate dominion

STUDY NOTES

The second creation story, and the human being's role in it, convey a sense of the vital power the land has over its creatures and of human submission to that power in the act of farming. The priestly writer of the first creation story views the human as master of the earth, while the Yahwist writer of the second sees him/her as its servant. Taken together, the two accounts show the human vocation, somewhat confusingly to our minds, as dominion, supervision, dependence and service. Human beings are made both in the image of God and from the dust of the earth.

The two Adams in Paul's teaching

The relationship between the two Adams was not seen as a problem in the Early Church. Paul used the two stories in his teaching on the resurrection: 1 Corinthians 15.44, 47, 49. This is important teaching, but it removes the force of the participatory, serving nature of the Yahwist's Adam character.

The two Adams in Augustine's teaching

Later conflations of the two accounts made the Yahwist Adam represent our lower, earthly nature: a disobedient man of dust. Augustine wrote:

What we need to understand is how a man can be called, on the one hand, the image of God and, on the other, is dust and will return to dust. The former relates to the rational soul which God by his breathing, or, better, by his inspiration communicated to man, meaning to the body of man; but the latter refers to the body such as God formed it from dust into the man to whom a soul was given . . . The soul is not the entire man, but only his better part; nor is the body the entire man, but merely his inferior part . . . [God] made man in his own image, for he created for him a soul endowed with reason and intelligence so that he might excel all the creatures of the earth, air, and sea which were not so gifted.[7]

Separation of spirit and matter

This philosophical dualism subsumed the Yahwist creation account into the priestly account. In the Church, the distinction between spirit and matter prevailed, taken up in medieval theology, and by the Cartesian separation of mind and matter. Indeed, Descartes offered humankind the prospect of becoming 'masters and possessors of the universe', a phrase that resonates uncomfortably with Genesis 1.26 and 28. Calvin wrote: 'God ordained all things for our profit and salvation', pointing out that Adam was created last of all, when everything had been made ready for him.[8]

Inappropriate dominion

In his famous article published in 1967, Lynn White claimed that Christianity was responsible for the current ecological crisis. He said that Christianity taught that it was God's will for man to exploit nature for his own purposes.[9]

The idea of human domination resonates with twentieth-century secular technological invasions of the natural order through pollution and damming of the water cycles, pollution of the atmosphere, attaining the status of rogue species and threatening other species in the biosphere, mining the rocky under-surface of the earth and over-cultivating its thin topsoil. Humans were top of the food-chain, the most evolved of all creatures.

Christianity could not be blamed for secularist dictators such as Stalin and Mao, who used science and technology to flex their muscles and show who was in charge, but the same idea of human dominion was playing itself out. The relentless pursuit of economic growth in the twentieth and twenty-first centuries keeps this idea firmly in place.

A man emerged from a car in Belgrave Square, a smart area in the centre of London. He was extremely well-dressed in a suit of soft grey material, and had a cashmere coat slung over his shoulders. His shoes were beautiful leather. The car was a chauffeur-driven Bentley. It had stopped on a double yellow line, and once the man was out, it drove off. He strode across the pavement to his destination: one of the large town houses that form the square in this wealthy part of town. He looked and behaved as though he was 'master and possessor of the universe'. His universe was arranged to his liking; he could command things to happen and they did.

There's a tale of a mouse who plagued a man in his house. The mouse seemed to grow bolder by the day, and no matter what the man did to try to rid himself of the mouse, he could not succeed. Then one day the man found the mouse's nest. It was piled high with stuff – bits and pieces the mouse had found in the house. The man cleared away the pile – and the mouse suddenly lost all his confidence and was soon trapped and killed. The moral of the story is that often confidence – the idea of being a master and possessor of the universe – comes with possessions. In fact, the confidence is vested in the possessions, not in the person. What, one wonders, would the man in Belgrave Square be like if he had no material wealth?

In penitence, we renounce our claim on possessions and the false sense of dominion that they give us. We learn what it means to be without.

SERMON POINTS

- Separating spirit and matter can make Christians think they only need to look after their own individual souls.
- Scientifically, matter can't be separated into hermetically sealed individual units; spiritually, neither can the divine source from which we all come. So, 'Who [and where] is my neighbour?'
- The Lenten fast of renunciation of possessions assists the removal of feelings of inappropriate dominion.

Penitence and renunciation 2: Choosing the right tree

STUDY NOTES

In the face of the consequences of uncontrolled human domination, in the form of too-fast heating of the earth, rising sea levels, and threats to numerous habitats of numerous species, some Christian theologies have tried to soften the dominion model of the first creation story. Consumerism and growth have not been questioned fundamentally, but the idea of dominion has been made more benevolent, often using the concept of stewardship. So rather than assuming a God-given right or even duty to dominate the things of nature for the good of humankind, humanity is to be reminded that creation is God's, and we are God's servants.

Stewardship, introducing the notion of service, and trustworthiness, is a very beautiful biblical concept. At no point in the Bible, however, does the term refer to the role of human beings in relation to the creation. Apart from some intriguing references in the Epistles, the word refers to a business relationship. The steward is a person of responsibility who is in charge of a household.

Stewardship in the Old Testament

In the Hebrew Scriptures there is no word for 'steward'; this is the English translation when the Hebrew phrase resembles something like 'one who has responsibility over a household'. Hence, in every context in the Hebrew Scriptures, the word describes the manager of a household and its effects: Genesis 24.2; 43.19; 1 Kings 16.9. There is at least one passage in the Hebrew Scriptures where the use of the word *rada* (dominion) could be translated as steward: Leviticus 25.43, 46, 53. In 1 Chronicles 28.1, the role of the steward as the manager of property is emphasized by its contrast with the other functionaries in David's household.

Stewardship in the New Testament

In the New Testament, the Greek word *oikonomenos* is translated as steward, or in some cases, manager. In the following single instance of a steward being in charge of something of the natural world, it is nevertheless the hiring and management of the workers, not the vines themselves, for which he is responsible: Matthew 20.8. The other two references in Luke are to household managers: Luke 12.42; 16.1ff. There is a reference in Romans to the steward as the one who cares for the finances of the city: Romans 16.23.

The other references in the Epistles (and the only other uses of *oikonomenos* in the Bible) take the meaning of the term to new and intriguing depths, but they still don't link stewardship with the natural world: 1 Corinthians 4.1–2; Galatians 4.2 (where it is the Christians themselves who are held in waiting to inherit their father's wealth) and Titus 1.7–9; 1 Peter 4.10 (where stewardship and teaching are connected).

Can human beings be stewards of creation?

The concept of stewardship is important, but it relates to responsible and trustworthy care of things over which human beings might be said to have some control. These things do not include the natural world. The idea of 'stewardship of creation', which is not biblical, retains lingering anthropocentric notions of being above, and in control of, the laws of nature. But we know that we are not in control. Who has ever been able to change the law of gravity, for example?

Stewardship of knowledge

We can think about the role of stewarding as relating to the way we handle the things over which we have control or should protect. Margaret Barker gives the example of the stewardship of knowledge, which involves looking beyond what the secular world has taught us to see. As an example, she points out the often-missed figure of Wisdom hidden in the Michelangelo painting of the creation of Adam, in the Sistine Chapel (the cloud the Creator sits in is shaped like a human brain and at the side of the Creator, in the centre of the brain, there is a dark-haired female figure). For Margaret Barker, stewardship of knowledge means knowing that the things on earth are as the things in heaven.[10]

Choosing the right tree

Stewardship, then, can be thought of in relation to knowledge, reconnecting knowledge with its divine origins. The references in the Epistles point to this second understanding of the term. Richard Chartres discusses the way in which Adam and Eve ate fruit from the wrong tree when they chose the tree of knowledge.[11] The tree of life, which was accessible to them in Paradise, was the tree of Wisdom, true knowledge about the divine creation (Proverbs 3.13-18) that brings healing to the nations (Revelation 22.2). Instead of eating from this tree, they chose the forbidden Tree of Knowledge, which

had the effect of distorting their perception of the creation and seeing it as separate and independent from its divine source.

SERMON POINTS

- A steward is responsible for that which he or she can control. Human beings cannot control the waves, but we control the knowledge that can, for example, make use of the power of the waves.
- Stewardship of knowledge means using our knowledge (scientific discoveries; artistic skills) wisely and for the good of all creatures.
- The choice of tree – the tree of knowledge of good and evil or the tree of Wisdom and life – determines how we perceive and therefore behave towards the world. But that means renouncing power.

Penitence and renunciation 3: Piercing the veil

STUDY NOTES

Symbolism of the holy of holies

Lent can be thought of as a journey into the holy of holies of the Temple. In Temple symbolism, this is the place whence creation arises, and in it the whole of creation is known about in a moment, rather as Mozart was said to have heard a whole symphony in one moment in his mind before he wrote it down. It is Day One of the creation, when God said, 'Let there be light.' It is a place of rest and resolution, containing everything. It is a place of blinding light, purifying fire. A person cannot see it and live as that individual again. The purifying fire changes the perception, changes what sees and what is seen or, rather, reveals what is really there. It is where the throne of the Lord rests. At the heart of the cosmic covenant is God, and by his presence all things are held in place. Understanding this at some deep level changes everything. It is the basis of our behaviour towards the environment because we recognize that everything in creation is connected to God.

What the veil was made of

In Lent we pierce the veil that hangs over the holy of holies and enter, at first, into darkness. The veil hung between the holy of holies, representing that which is beyond space and time, and the outer temple, representing the phenomenal creation. It was made of blue, purple and scarlet thread and white linen, and was embroidered with patterns of cherubim worked in gold (Exodus 26.31; 36.35; 2 Chronicles 3.14). Exodus 28.31-33 tells us that the priestly vestments were similarly worked. The veil was symbolic of the elements of the phenomenal creation: air, fire, water and earth. The gold of the cherubim represented the link between the visible and the invisible creation.

The veil as incarnation

The veil can be seen as the earliest expression of the Incarnation, for those who cannot bear the radical meaninglessness, invisibility and unconditionality of the world beyond the senses. Clement of Alexandria writes of Christ taking on the colours of the veil in the form of the priestly vestments, thus cloaking God in sensory garb and simultaneously concealing and revealing him.[12] In Hebrews, Jesus is described as passing through the veil, which is also his flesh: Hebrews 10.19-20. Mark 15.38 (and parallels) states that as Christ breathed his last: 'The curtain of the temple was torn in two, from top to bottom.' In the *Liturgy of James*, one of the most ancient liturgies of the Eastern Church and still in use, we read the following prayer:

> *We thank thee, O Lord our God, that thou hast given us boldness for the entrance of thy holy places, which thou hast renewed to us as a new and living way through the veil of the flesh of thy Christ. We therefore, being counted worthy to enter into the place of the tabernacle of thy glory, and to be within the veil, and to behold the holy of holies, cast ourselves down before thy goodness.*[13]

The veil conceals and reveals as the divine becomes visible when it is clothed in the material world. The Greek Septuagint version of Exodus 25.8 reads: 'Let them make a sanctuary that I may be seen among them.' Other references to God's canopy can be found in 2 Samuel 22.12; Psalms 18.11; 104.2; Isaiah 40.22. The veil indicates that God is present, just as a sheet thrown over a person will show the existence of someone who can't be seen; or a sound emanating from a person who is hidden will indicate their presence; or, as every author knows, characters will reveal themselves through what they say.

The veil as guardian of the holy of holies and of Paradise

The veil could be seen as synonymous with the guardian cherubim around the throne in the holy of holies. These were huge, their wings spanning the whole width of the sanctuary, thus acting like a curtain. As cherubim, they convey the chariot throne of God and guard the sanctuary. This resonates with the passage in Psalm 18.10-11. We are also reminded of the guardians of the garden of Eden (Genesis 3.24). Are they guarding Day One, Paradise, the holy of holies, and if so, why should they? From the outside it might seem, as it would have seemed to Adam and Eve, that the presence of the cherubim prevents entry. But they might also be seen as issuing an invitation, dancing through the weave of the visible world, if we could only see them and know what they are doing. The veil is like a trick, appearing and disappearing, something that seems a huge thing to step through, and yet was torn in two by Christ's death, becoming like gossamer as we pass through.

The veil as the human mind

Or is the veil the mind? Just as the Deuteronomists sought to constrain and control the cosmic covenant Temple tradition by ridding themselves of the mystical elements and creating a central control, and just as the Pharisees sought to fix and formulate the Law so as to keep it separate and special to their kind, so our minds try to understand and control things that are beyond their comprehension because they are beyond space and time and our minds always work in time. Hence, our minds draw a veil over God and create an imaginary gulf. Only by a leap of faith into Lenten darkness, which does not depend upon our minds' understanding, and does not rely on our minds' version of truth, can the veil be parted. The Transfiguration of Mark 9.2-8 pulled the disciples through the veil to a vision that their minds would not comprehend.

The veil as death

The veil is also death. At Christ's death, the ultimate death, the Temple curtain was torn in two. The self dies, and the veil parts.

The veil in Revelation

This positive/negative characterizing of the veil is supported by the anti-Temple vision in Revelation 17 in which the great harlot is seen clothed in scarlet and purple (a travesty of Mary, perhaps, because she is apocryphally said to have been weaving the scarlet and purple colours of the Temple veil when the Annunciation took place[14]) and decorated with gold and jewels. The veil is both invitation and barrier, depending on how it is seen.

Piercing the veil

> ... smyte upon that thicke cloude of unknowing with a scharp darte of longing loue, & go not thens for thing that befalleth.[15]

The perspective from the phenomenal creation or outer Temple is that the veil is like a gateway that has to be gone through, a hurdle, a boundary that is not easily crossed and possibly cannot be crossed on one's own or by one's own volition.

Christ's passing through the Temple veil opens the way for all. In the Temple ritual of the Day of Atonement, the high priest passed through the curtain with the blood of the sacrifice, which was then sprinkled on the curtain, cleansing and purifying creation, restoring its wholeness and fertility. Passing through the curtain is the leap of faith, the transcendental step that is not really a step and can hardly be described. The accounts of the transfiguration of Christ are helpful as we seek to understand this: Mark 9.2-8 and parallels. The disciples had a taste of what Jesus was in truth in that moment when he revealed himself to them beyond the curtain, beyond the veil of flesh, and garbed in divinity (in the Book of Enoch, angels are 'men in white', compare Acts 1.10). The presence of figures from the past indicates that in this moment we are beyond space and time.

Isaiah 40.22 is a vision from beyond the veil in which the inhabitants of the earth look like grasshoppers and the veil becomes the boundaries of the sanctuary.

And so the Lenten fast can be seen as a gradual piercing of the veil around the holy of holies as the supplicant slowly and penitentially learns to do without his 'outer garment' of possessions and actions, everything that he calls his own, and learns to stand naked before God. It is the ultimate lightening of one's footprint on the earth as one leaves behind all material longing and turns wholeheartedly, empty-handed, to the Divine, and steps through the veil. In a sermon for Lent, Richard Chartres said:

> The spiritual practice of the inner journey is hard and the dangers great, but the joy of seeing draws us on, although at times it is impossible to distinguish the joy from the agony.
>
> When I was young I knew everything. It was very exhausting. I was constantly defending my castle walls, labelling and judging what lay outside.
>
> Opposition hardened my position, but as George Herbert says in his great poem, 'Love bade me welcome,' and miraculously found a way through the defences. Jesus Christ, in his life and living Spirit, glimpsed in scriptures and in life, showed me that you must give self away in order to grow in soul.
>
> The crust once breached, I found that there was an answering call from within where the spiritual heart is in each one of us, where there is a centre deep within which connects with the centre of everything that lives.[16]

Monica Furlong said:

> I am clear what I want of the clergy. I want them to be people who can by their own happiness and contentment challenge my ideas about status, about success, about money, and so teach me to live more independently of such drugs. I want them to be people who can dare, as I do not dare, and as few of my contemporaries dare to refuse to work flat out (since work is an even more subtle drug than status) to refuse to compete with me in strenuousness. I want them to be people who are secure enough in the value of what they are doing to have time to read, to sit and think, and who can face the emptiness and possible depression which often attack people when they do not keep the surface of their mind occupied. I want them to be people who have faced this kind of loneliness and discovered how fruitful it is, as I want them to be people who have faced the problems of prayer. I want them to be people who can sit still without being guilty.[17]

SERMON POINTS

- Lent is a time to head with penitence and faith into the darkness of the holy of holies, knowing it may be some time before any light is revealed; rather like going into a tunnel without seeing the light at its end. But Christ entered before us and we can follow with confidence.
- Entering the holy of holies can be thought of as prayer, when the surface of the mind is no longer occupied and the supplicant has dared to refuse to work flat out.
- Penitence is a softening of a hard heart; the soft heart risks letting everything in, caring for all of creation.

LITURGICAL LINKS

- A full range of liturgical resources for Lent can be found in *Common Worship: Times and Seasons* (pages 211–56) and in *Together for a Season: Lent, Holy Week, Easter.*
- Further penitential material, including a Corporate Service of Penitence, is included in 'Reconciliation and Restoration: Recovering Baptism' from *Common Worship: Christian Initiation*, page 227ff.

Holy Week and Easter

Overarching theme:

Christ's salvation of humans is inseparable from his salvation of the rest of the earth

Practical themes:

- Flower stories
- Signs of life after death
- Ethical Easter eggs

Theological themes:

- The ecological symbolism of bread
- Crucifixion and resurrection as ecological paradigms
- Taking matter (earth) as seriously as spirit

Introductory meditations

Palm Sunday

Deep in your Lenten fast, accustomed to the darkness, content, by now, with solitude and simplicity, knowing, by now, your lack of dependency on material things, you are called to a strange, noisy celebration, asked to mingle with a crowd whose cheerful joshing you don't quite understand or share . . . until you see the source of their joy, and you join in, wholeheartedly cheering the King who is entering Jerusalem on – well, the incongruity of a donkey strikes a jarring or perhaps a warning note – and a palm leaf is thrust into your hands, except it's in the shape of a cross, and that is disturbing, too.

Date palms decorated the walls of the Temple and symbolized Paradise. The palm cross is a powerful image, drawing together the elements of the Christian story in one object taken from the natural world and fashioned by human hands.

Palm Sunday is undoubtedly a celebration, but it is one that demonstrates the mood swings of a volatile crowd – the crowd that will call for Jesus' blood only a few days later. The feeling here is as the feeling you have when you're partying with friends, consuming like mad, perhaps with very rich friends, with people who don't think about the consequences of their actions for the planet, and you are in absolutely no position to judge or separate yourself, not least because you are genuinely enjoying yourself and anyway these are your friends whom you love, but somewhere inside you there's an uncomfortable feeling and it is as much directed at yourself as it is at others. Hold that thought!

Maundy Thursday

The symbolism here – the footwashing, the institution of the Eucharist – demonstrates leadership as service. The priesthood is the antithesis to mistaken ideas of dominion and stewardship. Priests are leaders, but demonstrate their leadership through Wisdom, drawing people to God by setting themselves where their congregations are, and feeding their need. Footwashing is resonant with echoes of baptism. The bread of the Eucharist was prefigured by the bread of the Presence in Solomon's Temple, where it was linked with atonement.

Good Friday

Popular devotion concentrates on identifying with the suffering of Christ. But as David Stancliffe points out, the formal liturgy celebrates the triumph of the cross with the cry *tetelestai*, 'it is finished', or more accurately, 'it is perfectly accomplished'.[1] The image of the seed sown in darkness is evoked: 'Very truly, I tell you, unless a grain of wheat falls into the earth and dies, it remains just a single grain; but if it dies, it bears much fruit' (John 12.24).

The fruit of the tree of death, freely given, reverses the wrong choice made in the garden of Eden, and the tree of death becomes the tree of life.[2]

Easter Eve

Jesus really died. In some Orthodox churches, a funeral service is held for Jesus, using his name at all the appropriate moments. In other churches, the Eucharist is celebrated but stops short at the Lord's Prayer. This demonstrates the power of liturgy to tell a story and provoke a response in its participants. The effect of such liturgies must be profound. Jesus really died. Saturday is a dead time, a time of waiting, and watching, and not knowing.

Jesus really died. So, too, do the things of nature. The seasonal shift from autumn to winter causes the land and the creatures to go quiet and disappear. The trees lose their leaves and look dead, and hard frost or a blanket of snow, or heavy rains and endless grey skies try to persuade us that the end has come and nothing will live again. It's hard to imagine spring in the depths of winter. It's impossible to imagine that someone who died will live again. Jesus really died.

Easter Day

And he is risen. Mary goes to the tomb to look for a dead body to anoint, and finds *adam* – a gardener – sowing a seed, the second Adam, risen from the *adamah* and serving it still.

Practical ideas for Holy Week and Easter
Colour: white or gold

The Christian year moves on: 'Ride on, ride on in majesty', as the Palm Sunday hymn resounds. The story must be one of the most well known of all stories, and over the centuries Christians have held on to their palms as a simple link with that awesome journey.

Pussy-willow was the usual substitute for the palms of the Holy Land, but when Easter was late, the yew tree provided an alternative. Henry VIII supported the use of the yew as a palm, but his son did not and the term 'Palm Sunday' was excluded from the Book of Common Prayer in 1552. How things can change, but then isn't that the message of Palm Sunday?

And so follows Holy or **Passion Week**, which was once known as the Great Week, starting with the Great Sabbath. This week was an opportunity to 'increase labours, fastings, watching, giving more liberal alms and generally testifying the greatness of the divine goodness of their care of good works and more intense piety and holy living.'[3]

Holy Week customs and rituals

On Maundy Thursday, the monarch gives coins to the elderly, the total number of coins corresponding to the monarch's age; the clergy wash the feet of some members of the congregation; and altars are stripped and then washed with wine and water and rubbed with herbs.

THE STORY TOLD IN A FLOWER

Simply stand with amazement and glory in the intricacies of the Passion flower (*passiflora*): you can tell the story from the flower in the palm of your hand:

the leaf – the spear
five petals and five sepals – the ten apostles (excluding Peter and Judas)
five anthers – the five wounds
the tendrils – the scourges
the column of the ovary – the pillar of the cross
three stigmas – the three nails
the filaments within the flower – the crown of thorns
the calyx – the glory or nimbus
the white tint – purity
the blue tint – heaven

The whole flower keeps open for three days, symbolizing the three years' ministry of Christ.

The Synoptics tell us that the Last Supper was the Passover meal or *pesach* (from which we derive our word 'paschal'). At this time of the year, nature gives us the **Pasque flower** (*pulsatilla vulgaris*) – a rare native plant with yellow stamens and purple petals in the shape of a bell, which is only found on chalk grasslands in central and eastern England. It was, of course, a purple robe in which the soldiers dressed Jesus.

It is claimed that during the time of the Crusades, a bishop brought several yew trees back from the **garden of Gethsemane** and that the ancient yew growing at Rycroft Manor in Oxfordshire is one of these trees, having been planted there by the bishop in 1135. There is little or no evidence, however, to suggest that yews grew among the olive trees in Gethsemane.

The Holy Thorn of Glastonbury (see page 27), which blossoms at Christmas, will blossom again at this time.

SIGNS OF LIFE AFTER DEATH

Anthony Foottit, in his *A Gospel of Wild Flowers*, reminds us that the old name for primrose was Easter rose. Primroses are truly the heralds of spring – the pale flowers reflect the first sunshine of the new season and the deeper yellow at the centre reminds us of the summer to come. In contrast to Passion flowers, primroses could not be simpler, but Anthony encourages us to look at them carefully. They are not common or garden flowers but are full of glory.

Let's hope there will be enough primroses to make some posies to be hung on those Lenten crosses, recycled from Christmas trees, as a symbol of life starting after death.

A MOVEABLE FEAST

Easter is the original 'moveable feast', so called because it can be any time between 22 March and 25 April. In 2008, bar one day, Easter was the earliest it ever can be. It only falls on such an early date once every hundred years. Unlike February daffodils, it has nothing to do with global warming. Easter Day is always the first Sunday after the paschal full moon on or after the spring equinox (20 or 21 March). If the full moon falls on a Sunday, then Easter is the next Sunday.

We don't know when Christians first began to make this annual memorial of the death and resurrection of Christ, but the fact that the dating of Easter was fixed according to the Jewish lunar calendar, whereas every other Christian feast depends on the solar calendar, suggests that the custom, like the observance of Sunday, the day of resurrection, was already established in apostolic days. It is the Christian Passover.

THE EASTER EGG HUNT

Organizing an Easter egg hunt? Remember that you can buy fair-trade mini eggs made with Kasmithula sugar from Malawi and cocoa from Ghana. The eggs are produced by Kuapa Kokoo, a co-op union of 937 village societies, which represents about 40,000 farmers, who sell about 650 tonnes of cocoa to the fair-trade market each year. The village of Kapasule in Malawi now has its own supply of safe, clean water from a borehole paid for by the fair-trade premium.

Study notes and sermon points for Holy Week and Easter

As we move from crucifixion to resurrection during Holy Week, we can gain a deeper understanding of new life in ourselves, in creation, and through Christ, as part of our growing understanding of God's planet and our place in it.

New life 1: Maundy Thursday and the bread of the Presence

STUDY NOTES

Bake bread

At a dialogue at St Paul's Cathedral in a series called 'Costing the earth? The quest for sustainability' the Jain ecologist Satish Kumar answered a question about what we should do in the face of ecological crisis by saying that we should 'bake bread':

> Practical, meditative. Baking bread. It becomes a spiritual practice. It becomes a symbol of sustainable, ecological lifestyle, when we start to make things rather than consume, consume, consume. We are not consumers, we are makers of things. So, baking bread will be a good start.[4]

The Eucharistic bread

Martin Warner has pointed out that the transformation of our understanding to seeing the things of the earth as a gift from God, for which we are profoundly grateful, rather than as objects of choice for our consumption, happens at the Eucharist, instituted on Maundy Thursday: 'In contrast to our culture of waste, God provides the meal that satisfies every desire with "all dainties".'[5]

The offertory prayer links the things of the adamah, earth, with the work of human hands and the transforming power of God:

> Blessed are you, Lord God of all creation:
> through your goodness we have this bread to set before you,
> which earth has given and human hands have made.
> It will become for us the bread of life.[6]

Bread in the Temple

The bread offering in the Temple was an important part of its ritual. The Hebrew lehem panim means literally 'the bread of the Face' or 'Presence'. The texts indicate that the bread was thought of as the presence of the Lord: see, for example, Malachi 1.6c-7a. An early Coptic Jacobite prayer asks: 'Make your face shine on this bread and cup.'[7] In several passages 'presence' is taken to mean 'self', and this is emphasized by the Septuagint translation, which has the Greek word autos (self): Exodus 33.14; Deuteronomy 4.37; Isaiah 63.9. Jesus Christ, Israel's ruler, was to come from the house of bread – beth lehem: Micah 5.2.

The bread of the Presence was most holy and could only be eaten by the priests. Eating the bread was one of two exclusive acts of the priests; the other was to take the blood of the sacrifice into the holy of holies on the Day of Atonement, prefiguring the Eucharist. As Christ was both the High Priest and the sacrifice, opening to all the way to the holy of holies, so David's act of eating the exclusive bread anticipated Christ making the bread available to all.

Give us today the bread of tomorrow

The word for 'daily bread', *epiousios*, is a very rare word and its meaning is uncertain. Commenting on this, Margaret Barker quotes Jerome (d. AD 420):

> In the Hebrew Gospel according to Matthew, it is thus: 'Our bread of the morrow, give us this day.' This is reflected in the canonical Matthew: 'Give us today the *epiousios* bread.'[8]

In his commentary on Matthew 6.11, Jerome says that the Hebrew word was *mahar*, 'tomorrow', a word which to the early Christians meant the coming of the kingdom of heaven, and therefore had a powerful significance. So the invocation in the Lord's Prayer was not simply that we should be fed, but that we should receive the bread of the Presence that was the Lord.

Christ as the bread of life

Chapter 6 of John's Gospel is the description *par excellence* of Christ as the bread of life. It begins with the feeding of the five thousand, in which five barley loaves are transformed into twelve baskets of fragments. In the Temple, twelve loaves were placed on the table as an offering. The miracle persuades the people that Jesus is indeed the prophet they are expecting, but he outmanoeuvres them when they attempt to turn him into a political and earthly king, and disappears into the holy of holies, symbolized as a mountain.

Christ then performs the miracle of walking on water. In Temple symbolism, the bronze basin of water, known as 'the sea', that filled the outer courtyard, had to be passed before the Temple could be entered. By walking on the water before the disciples and leading them to the other side, Christ is opening the way into the Temple for all.

Then the disciples ask questions about the bread. Jesus points out that the manna brought to the Israelites in the wilderness was from God, not from Moses (thus removing the idea that there is an intermediary step, via the Law, to God). In the following passage, Christ identifies himself with the bread, thus, once again, embodying a Temple symbol and making it available to all — if they are prepared to 'eat' him: John 6.33-35, 37, 39, 51.

Eating the bread

The action of David in eating the bread of the Presence in the Temple is linked with the action of Christ. David is given five loaves of the bread of the Presence: Christ is given five loaves to share among the 5,000. Both offer the most holy bread to others than the priests. The bread, the presence of God in the form of Wisdom, is to be eaten, thus making those who eat it wise. Christ extends the meaning of this: it is his body that is to be eaten, but only by those who are sent by the Father. By eating his body, the people are called together to the Father as one body, which, Christ says, is his work on the earth.

SERMON POINTS

- By speaking the Lord's Prayer, we are asking for his kingdom to come now: 'Give us this day the bread of tomorrow.'
- By participating in the Eucharist, we become one with the body of Christ.
- By baking bread, we become makers, not consumers.

New life 2: Good Friday reflection[9]

This meditation can be used privately or as part of worship or as a group meditation. It links the events of Good Friday with environmental concern.

First voice   It's Good Friday. Today we hold our breath, for today we don't know about the Resurrection, we only know that Christ has died. Today, we die with him, and we don't know what is going to happen next. Today, we have stopped being busy, running around and organizing and rearranging the world and each other. Today, we are uncertain about everything. Today, we can't explain how the world works or what our function in it might be. Today, we have been silenced. Caught in profound unknowing, we sit still, untriumphant. Today, we are the seed that falls to the ground, dead, and is buried deep in the soil.

Second voice   As we prepare to celebrate Easter, Christians recall that through Christ the whole of creation is reconciled or restored to God, and that this places a moral or ethical imperative upon us. To continue to live in a relationship to creation that is distorted, to subject ourselves to all manner of structures and systems that cause us to utilize the planet in a way that destroys it, is completely contrary to the gospel. At the very least, we're called to be good stewards of that which is given to us in trust for our children and their children.

First voice   Think about the cross, symbol of our Christian faith. Think of the horizontal bar as symbolizing your journey through life, and now think of the vertical bar as the present moment. The present moment is a kind of death. Death is present in life, every moment. So when you re-embark on your journey, after Good Friday is over and the world starts up again and you breathe normally again, don't think of only the start of the journey and the finish of the journey as your resting place, think of the places in between as you go on your way, each footfall a measure of the vertical bar of the cross, each moment now your concern, your home.

Second voice   Think of the cross and what it was made of. Some say it would have been made of oak for oak trees were plentiful in Judea. Others maintain that four different woods were used – cedar, palm, olive and cypress. Cypress is planted in cemeteries in the Holy Land – the funeral tree, its dark, tall, waving plumes render it peculiarly appropriate among the tombs in sharp contrast to the plants growing elsewhere, where the combined heat and dryness of the climate forms the thorns used to make his crown.

First voice   Later he was to appear in a garden, not perhaps the type of garden we would know. The oldest trees in the garden of Gethsemane were olives. After their blossoms in spring the coolness of the pale blue foliage, the evergreen freshness, spread like a silver sea along the slopes and hills – a sign of peace and plenty, food and gladness.

Second voice	The trunk of the olive, gnarled and wrinkled, often hollow and scathed, yet yielding abundant crops to the extremest old age and renewing itself from the inside, suggests the idea of perpetual youth continuing to provide oil for lamps, cooking, soap and wood for fine furniture – no wonder it was used to make the cherubim, doors and posts for the Temple of Solomon.
First voice	But the olive when not tended soon ceases to yield a crop.
Second voice	So what has faith to do with the environment? Everything. Humans have despoiled the environment because they have used it functionally. They have not seen it – and therefore loved it – for what it is, but only for what it can do for them.
First voice	Repentance is, literally, turning around. Now is the time, when we are stripped of all certainties and prejudices and explanations, to look afresh at the creation and our relationship with it. Anything will do – a tree, another person, your own hand, a cup, a blade of grass, you'll find it's really very beautiful, just as it is. It's unique. There isn't another one exactly like it anywhere in the universe. No two blades of grass are the same.
Second voice	After the deep contemplation Good Friday has called us to, our perception of the earth should change for ever. And so should the way we live, because perception determines behaviour.

New life 3: Easter Sunday: Reuniting spirit and matter

STUDY NOTES

The resurrection of Christ confounds our sense of the difference between physical and spiritual. Jesus himself rose; not a spirit leaving a body behind. The earth itself is caught up in the salvation of Christ.

Adam and *adamah*

The Resurrection could make us reconsider the connection between the man and the dust from which he was drawn in the Yahwist account of creation. St Francis understood it, and so did the Irish monks and the Benedictines. By its nature, it is a humbler view, however, and would never have fought for dominance. Its voice is being heard more readily now, not least through the vehicle of a much-needed feminist theology that does not impose hierarchies on nature and recognizes the limits of human capacity. The Yahwist model offers an understanding of the inter-relationship of all created things and does not separate spirit and matter. It sees life breathing through all things and impresses a radical equality based on interdependence.

The farmer has to tune into the earth if s/he wishes to be fed by it. The so-called green revolution of the post-war years achieved, through the use of chemical fertilisers, a tremendous boost in crop production, but in the end the use of chemicals had to be restrained and the rhythm and natural fertility of the soil had to be rediscovered and respected if the soil was not to become sterile. The farmer knows the land cannot in the end be subdued, and also knows – as city dwellers may be prone to forget – that there is no such thing as a post-agrarian society. If the land goes, humankind goes with it. Ironically, and tragically, our domination may bring us to precisely this realization that, in the end, we *are* the servants of the land – if we succeed in destroying its fertility to the point where the self-organizing Gaian system rebels and humankind is destroyed for the sake of the whole planet's survival.

Appropriate dominion

Should we be choosing between the two accounts of creation? Is the priestly account wrong, and the Yahwist account right (or vice versa)? We don't have to be so absolutist in our thinking. Margaret Barker's interpretation of *rada* and *kabas* is altogether more benign. It affords a role to humanity that takes our ability to transform the natural world seriously, but gives a context and direction to the work that is altogether in the model of the servant. She points us to Psalm 8, in which humankind is given dominion, but only because we have looked up at the stars and seen how small we are in comparison with the glory of the heavens: 'This Adam is no strong ruler, trampling the earth; this is the shepherd king or the gardener.'[10]

Not just personal morality

The problem with the priestly dominion theology was that it subsumed the Yahwist theology, aided by the separation of spirit and matter and the glorifying of spirit over matter. Christians have looked to their immortal souls and their own personal morality, and failed to see the wide world living by God's breath, his name in and through all the earth. We have not understood our total dependence on the aerial ocean we ourselves breathe every moment of our lives. We have been separated from the soil on which we depend for food and shelter. We haven't known that the tears that fall from our eyes and the rain that falls from the sky are one circling flow of water through the planet and through our bodies: 'Humanity, despite its artistic pretensions, its sophistication and its many accomplishments, owes its existence to a six inch layer of topsoil and the fact that it rains.'[11]

Perceiving aright

The following passage is inspirational because it speaks of the total participation of the person in the creation, and also the perception of the unity of God that lies beyond and through it. It is an expression of the unity of spirit and matter. It is a human being fulfilling his function to serve and guard the creation by uniting with it and perceiving the Wisdom that holds it. And, like a seer or a prophet, he has spoken of what he has seen:

I came across it on a lonely country lane close to midnight. I was walking under a starlit sky with moonlight bathing a patchwork of fields in shades of black and white. I watched a warm breeze frisk a vast carpet of ripening wheat. It sent waves rippling across the surface to eddy around a line of ink-black oaks . . . I stood there motionless, listening intently and thinking of nothing, just letting the stillness of the night well around me.

After about ten minutes my blunt intrusion began to melt into the surroundings. After another ten minutes . . . things began to move. First, a scampering of tiny feet cut a dash in front of me. Then more came, smaller and faster this time, desperately ducking and diving through the tall green stalks, almost shouting 'Wait for me!' A hedgehog snuffled by. I caught the light-footed shadow of a young fox picking its way across a meadow towards a copse where, on the verge of the darkness, the flick of a tail betrayed the long legs of a deer. Before my eyes the quiet night became a teeming world, and I immersed myself in the subtle cacophony it made. It was then that I heard something I was not expecting, something which blew my mind.

It was precipitated by the ghostly white shadow of a barn owl which swept across the field making no sound at all. Immediately it silenced everything. I, too, held my breath as the hairs on the back of my neck bristled. I stood wide-eyed, on total alert, aware of everything. I felt completely plugged into the universe, but it still came as a shock when I suddenly sensed another layer. It was as if this entire orchestra of activity around me, the scrabbling of creatures, the creak and bend of branches and the swish and sway of the corn, had all lifted as one and separated from the sound that lay beneath, what I can only describe as a bedrock of absolute silence. Not a deadness, not an absence of sound, but a solid silence projecting a benign presence that inundated my senses completely. It rang in my ears. It still does now in my memory. But it was gone as quickly as it came, extinguished by the sudden fizz of my thoughts.[12]

Alienation and restoration

For most of us, the feeling of being master and possessor of the universe is a pretty alien one. Indeed, the consequence of bad eco-theology, for most of us, has not been deliberate exploitation of the natural world, except by extension – the lives we lead and the economic systems of which we are a part tend to make us live profligately. The consequence of bad eco-theology has been, in point of fact, alienation and a terrible loneliness. Cut off from our natural roots, unaware of the deep evolutionary kinship we have with all the earth and all the living organisms that are part of the earth-system, we wonder if we have a place in the universe at all, if there is anything we can do to deserve that place. Two poems by Mary Oliver may be helpful: 'Wild Geese' (Wild Geese: Selected Poems, Bloodaxe Books, 2004) is for those of us who are lonely; 'Rice' (New and Selected Poems, Beacon Press, 1992) helps to connect us to the land where our food comes from.

SERMON POINTS

- The resurrection of Christ is salvific for all creation.
- Human beings will always need land for food. There is no such thing as a post-agrarian society.
- Waiting on creation rather than trying to do things to it can bring about a real experience or sense of God as its true inwardness.
- Connecting with the land means connecting with our kin.

LITURGICAL LINKS

- Creative worship resources for Holy Week and Easter may be found in *Together for a season: Lent, Holy Week and Easter*. These support the provision in *Common Worship: Times and Seasons*.

- For resources around the theme of bread, see the provision in *Common Worship: Times and Seasons* for Maundy Thursday (pages 293ff.) and Corpus Christi (pages 514ff.).

Ascension and Pentecost

Overarching theme:
The Holy Spirit fills the whole diverse creation

Practical themes:
- 50/50
- Sharing environmental concern
- Think global
- Offsetting

Theological themes:
- Holy of holies teaches the divine origin of creation
- Human beings as priests of creation

Introduction

Biblical time is neither linear nor cyclical but is in constant touch with eternity as the spokes of a wheel are connected to the hub. We sense it as 'now and not yet'. The Ascension has Christ entering the holy of holies, where God is seated, beyond time and place, Day One, beyond creation and always present. At the heart of the turning world is blinding light; the source of all creation; the place where all creation is held together as one; all diversity, all at once, as one.

As Jesus departs, the Holy Spirit descends and fills the whole earth: 'It is to your advantage that I go away, for if I do not go away, the Advocate will not come to you; but if I go, I will send him to you' (John 16.7).

As David Stancliffe points out, Pentecost is the counter to the Tower of Babel.[1] At Pentecost, there are diverse tongues, but they are all speaking one truth. They manifest the truth, known in the holy of holies, that all creation is held together as one in Christ.

In reflecting on the meaning of Ascension and Pentecost, we can bring to mind the complete diversity of creation. Every single human being is unique – even those who share genetic identity, having come from the same embryo, still have unique features. And so is every blade of grass. Recognizing this seeming infinity of diversity, or rather, the endless creativity of God, we can only marvel at its holding together as it does. The truth hidden in the holy of holies, where God is, is the key to the covenantal dance of creation. James Lovelock has hypothesized about the self-regulating organism that is the planet Earth; cosmologists look further to the galaxies and the ancient, empty, cold cosmos that made life possible. Nothing is disconnected. The ancient teaching of the Temple told this story; science is catching up.

The sacrament of creation, so described because at Pentecost the Holy Spirit fills the whole earth, means that there is no part of the earth that is not loved by God and revered by us. There is nowhere called 'away' where we can throw things. We reverence matter because through it we are saved. The Word became flesh and dwelt among us.

In complexity and size, human beings stand halfway between the micro-world and the cosmos. It takes roughly the same number of atoms to make a human as it would human bodies (theoretically) to make a star. With the coming of the Advocate, sent by Christ upon his Ascension to the holy of holies, came the responsibility of human beings to use their God-given talents and skills wisely. This is not to claim godlike status over other creatures, it is simply to recognize that we have capacity and we have to use that capacity in a way that does no harm. This requires us first to follow Christ into the holy of holies and understand the truth underlying the creation, thence to emerge and to treat it accordingly, and to teach others to do so. In the symbolism of the Temple, we live liturgically, that is to say, having seen its divine source, we treat the world as a sacred reality.

Practical ideas for Pentecost
Colour: red

Pentecost, which marks the coming of the Holy Spirit, is a time when 'the Church looks outwards and considers again its mission in the world'.[2] It may therefore be a good time to help our congregations look outwards and think about how we can work with others to bring about environmental change in the local community and beyond.

50/50

The word 'Pentecost' means 'fiftieth' and was the name given to the Jewish celebration of the fiftieth day after Moses had received the Law. It was because of this festival that all the disciples were together – and the rest is history. So can we use the number **50** to make something for our own time?

- Could a congregation of 50 be given a challenge, which individually they could do, but which could be increased 50 fold?
- Could all those aged 50 be given a challenge?
- An environmental audit with 50 questions may be a mammoth task, but the Shrinking the Footprint audit will give you 22 questions and they only cover energy issues (see Appendix 5).

SHARING ENVIRONMENTAL CONCERN: WORKING WITH YOUR COMMUNITY

It's easy to speak, not always easy to listen. Some years ago, Canon David Wyatt had the idea of creating a garden at his church in Salford. The church was a Victorian gem surrounded by some of the worst examples of **inner city deprivation**. The site had been a school playground and the first job was to clear the hardcore. Volunteers were needed and David recruited some of the toughest youngsters in the parish, who were usually involved in making the environment worse rather than improving it. Next came the earthwork and eventually the planting.

In time, the garden appeared and many of the residents in the high rises around, who could see the garden from their windows, began thinking that they could create one, too. And so they asked the local council if they could use the land around their flats. The officials were not prepared to listen to such ideas and answered the request by stating that the land was needed for parking cars. The people asked their priest to help and, being a campaigner, Canon Wyatt fought for their cause.

Not content with creating a garden, the locals drew up plans for a community orchard, and while this was developing, another idea for a residents' café started to take shape. Eventually, instead of being a place of urban despondency, the block with its orchard, garden and café had a waiting list of would-be residents. The people had been inspired and had spoken, and eventually their message was heard and a miracle happened in Salford.

If you were to add questions about the churchyard, the kitchen and transport, you would soon have your 50 questions.

- Or you could use your copy of *How Many Lightbulbs Does It Take to Change a Christian?* Five groups of ten could be involved.
- You might organize a project incorporating 50/50 in the title: one possibility, for instance, would be the launch of a car-share club.

Sharing environmental concern: working with other faiths

We could also mark the disciples' speaking in tongues by talking with those who, though they may not be of our faith, also share our concern for the environment. Most faiths are now taking environmental issues very seriously, and so these could set an agenda for meetings at local, national or even international levels. This could be the time to meet with others to discuss opportunities for the Abrahamic faiths to celebrate A Time for God's Creation. (Details of faith groups can be found in Appendix 2.)

OFFSETTING

Offsetting should be easy for most churches as so many parishes and dioceses are twinned with communities where climate change is already having a great effect. For example, the Diocese of Wakefield in Yorkshire, which is twinned to Mara in Tanzania, has raised £7,700 to fund a tree-planting project on a 300-acre site in the village of Iharara. Members of Wakefield congregations have raised over £7,000 by offsetting their energy use.

Here's how the Wakefield diocese calculated its carbon offsetting (the figures on the right indicate how much each person gives to offset their energy use):

A flight to Europe	£5 per person
A flight to Africa	£14
A flight to USA	£14
A flight to Australia	£30
Annual domestic energy use in a family house of 4 people	£50
Annual domestic energy use of a typical parish church	£90
Car use	50 pence per 100 miles
Train use	50 pence per 300 miles

For more information see ***www.wakefield.anglican.org/maratrees***.

Think global

Pentecost would be a good time to think about twinned dioceses and parishes. How will climate change affect things there? Have we studied their environment to know what it is really like? Do we have expertise that would help them? Do they need help with projects? Organizations like Christian Aid and Tearfund have information about different countries – see Appendix 2. Could we help to provide them with something they may be praying for that we may well take for granted? Rather than sending money to a commercial **Carbon Offsetting** company, why not set up a scheme for your parish or diocese to help a project directly? (An example of how to do this is given in the box opposite.)

There has been criticism of many commercial companies that offer offsetting services, but a scheme created by the Christian environmental organization A Rocha is committed to meeting the exacting standards of the Climate Community Biodiversity Alliance (***www.climate-standards.org***). Climate Stewards (a branch of A Rocha) encourages people first to *stop* producing so much carbon and only after that to *swap* their inevitable carbon dioxide emissions through offsetting.[3]

Study notes and sermon points for Ascension and Pentecost

At Ascensiontide, we remember Christ's return to the Father and the liberating effect on his disciples as the Holy Spirit enters them. The change in perception that bursting free from the old way of life brings us results in our seeing that the creation is truly of and from God.

Bursting free 1: Ascension and the holy of holies

STUDY NOTES

When he had said this, as they were watching, he was lifted up, and a cloud took him out of their sight. While he was going and they were gazing up towards heaven, suddenly two men in white robes stood by them. They said, 'Men of Galilee, why do you stand looking towards heaven? This Jesus, who has been taken up from you into heaven, will come in the same way as you saw him go into heaven.'

Acts 1.9-11

Holy of holies in Temple imagery

The holy of holies was the inner sanctuary of the Temple in Jerusalem. It is, symbolically, beyond time and space. It is where, so to speak, God sits, on the throne of the ark, guarded or supported by vast cherubim whose wings can be understood as the Temple veil protecting the sanctuary. The holy of holies is the place of transformation, of changed perception, of understanding the underlying unity of all things. On the Day of Atonement, the high priest would take the blood of atonement, the bread of the Presence, the oil and the incense (indicated in the passage above by the 'cloud') into the holy of holies and it would be transformed, becoming infectiously holy.

Priests themselves, entering the holy of holies, would have their own perception transformed, and they would re-emerge into the phenomenal creation to teach the truth about God as the source of all creation. Their vestments reflected this: in the outer temple, they wore robes of blue, white, scarlet and purple, like the Temple veil itself, while in the holy of holies they wore only white. In the holy of holies the cosmic covenant of interdependence is understood, and that understanding feeds the whole of one's life, the way one leads it, the way one relates to every other person or thing in it, and the way one speaks about the creation to others.

The holy of holies can be thought of in several different ways in relation to the environment. It is the place from which creation springs, and where the profound Wisdom is found that sees all things as interconnected and held together by God's eternal covenant. It can be thought of as the Sabbath, entered into by means of complete rest and retreat, leaving land fallow, ceasing work. For Christians, it is the place made open to all by the perfect atoning sacrifice of Christ, whose death tore the veil asunder. In Temple theology, the outer temple represents the phenomenal creation. Jesus' sacrificial entry into the holy of holies was atonement for the healing of the whole creation.

Biblical references to the holy of holies

Texts in the Bible that refer to this high sanctuary from which the whole world springs or can be seen include Job 38.4; Proverbs 8.22ff.; Isaiah 6.1ff.; 40.21ff.; Luke 4.5, 9; John 3.12-13; 8.23; Ephesians 1.9-10. It contains the whole of creation in potential and is therefore identified with the cosmic Christ: John 1.1-18; Colossians 1.15ff.

A place of light

The holy of holies is a place of light. The light is too great for someone to see it and live, as Moses was told (Exodus 33.20), and this fits with the sense of the holy of holies being a place you enter only when you leave all that you call yourself behind. But Second Isaiah wrote of the glory of the Lord rising, and followers of Jesus beheld his glory, so some have seen the light. Other passages speak of the light or fire of the holy of holies: Psalm 31.16; 50.2-3; 67.1; compare Numbers 6.24ff; Psalm 80.3; 104.2; Isaiah 9.2; 33.14, 17; 60.1; Daniel 7.9-10.

As well as the passage in John 1.14, the description of the Transfiguration (Mark 9.1-8) indicates that three of Jesus' disciples saw the light of the holy of holies. Other New Testament passages confirm that this light of the holy of holies is set free for Christians: John 17.5; 1 John 1.5ff; Ephesians 5.8, 14.

A place of judgement and purification

The holy of holies is also a place of judgement and purification (see Psalm 82.6-7; Isaiah 43.27-28; 66.6; Ezekiel 28 and elsewhere).

How is the sanctuary entered?

Job 28.23-24 hints at an answer. Christ opened the way to the holy of holies by his ultimate sacrifice. In the original Feast of the Atonement in Solomon's Temple, the high priest entered the holy of holies, taking the blood of the scapegoat with him, to atone for the sins of the people and to heal and renew the creation. By being taken into the holy of holies, as we have seen, the blood became infectiously holy, meaning that whatever it touched also became holy. The high priest would emerge with the blood and sprinkle the outer Temple with it, symbolizing the cleansing and restoration of the whole creation, the restoration of the cosmic covenant.

Jesus Christ entered the holy of holies as both High Priest and scapegoat, so his sacrifice was for all people, for the whole creation, for all eternity: Hebrews 9. The sprinkling of the outer temple with the infectiously holy blood of the scapegoat, which was for the healing of the earth, can be understood in Christian terms as the Holy Spirit 'sprinkling' herself over all the earth (water is one of the ways she is signified) at Pentecost, Christ having ascended to the *debir* (the inner Temple or holy of holies) as the High Priest and scapegoat.

At the Ascension, Jesus stepped out of space and time and entered eternity. In so doing he opened the way, through the Holy Spirit, for all creation to follow him. The flow of the Spirit through Ascension to Pentecost is unbreakable. Stepping into the holy of holies is stepping into the glory of God that underlies the whole creation. It is a making naked so as to be clothed in light, to have one's face shine in reflecting the glory of God, facing the sun.

SERMON POINTS

- Vision from the holy of holies shows the interconnectedness of all creation.
- It is beyond space and time so there can be no individual perception from it.
- Christ opened the way to it for all, for all time.

Bursting free 2: Pentecost and the priesthood of humanity

STUDY NOTES

Humanity's response to God

Participation in the Wisdom of God is the way to Paradise regained, an opportunity to choose the fruit from the tree of life, and not the tree of knowledge. This participation is through 'public work [which] is what the word liturgy means'.[4] Following Pentecost and the visitation of the Spirit, the call to be a priesthood of humanity is laid upon Christians. They are to take the light of Christ to the furthest ends of the earth and proclaim the truth about creation. This liturgical work treats the world as a sacred reality.

The holy of holies burst open

David Stancliffe speaks of the feast of Pentecost being the counterpart to the Tower of Babel. In the one case (Genesis 11.1-9), the utter diversity of people makes them fall apart from one another, incapable of communitarian behaviour. In the second (Acts 2.1-6), people learn to speak in one another's tongues and the channels of communication – and communion – are opened. Tongues of flame evoke images of the Temple. It is as though the light and fire of the holy of holies reaches now to the disciples, having been burst open by the priestly sacrifice of Christ. The Wisdom of God holds all the manifest diversity and uniqueness of the creation together and the vision of the holy of holies is of that unifying love running through everything, drawing it together and to God.

Retreat into silence

At Pentecost, the work of the followers of Christ begins. Humanity itself, imbued with the Holy Spirit, must assume priesthood. Roles assigned to priests in the old Temple tradition can guide us. In the Temple, the high priest wears pure white when he enters the holy of holies, and when he is in the outer temple he wears vestments of blue, scarlet, purple and white linen, reflecting the colours of the Temple veil. The symbolism is that of being clothed in flesh in the temporal world, the visible creation, and clothed in light like the angels when in the *debir* beyond the veil, beyond space and time, in the invisible creation. One commentary on the expulsion of Adam and Eve from Paradise is that the leaves that God gave them to cover themselves up were in fact clothes of flesh.[5] We enter the *debir* for the transformation of our perception and for understanding of the underlying unity of all things, and we emerge to see and speak of this unity in the outer Temple or phenomenal creation.

This making a retreat into silence can be experienced in many ways: prayer; Sabbath rest; contemplation; a walk in the rain; silence; a moment of sudden clarity visited quite unexpectedly in the middle of a busy street or a crowded room. D. H. Lawrence wrote: 'I have been dipped again in God, and new-created.'[6]

CONTEMPLATION

The contemplative tradition within Christianity is full of references that point the Christian disciple to the *debir*. Many contemplatives used the system of meditation on a word or a short prayer, such as the Jesus prayer of the Orthodox pilgrim, or this advice from the author of *The Cloud of Unknowing*:

> . . . take thee bot a litil worde of o silable; for so it is betir then of two, for euer the shorter it is, the betir it acordeth with the werk of the spirite, & soche a worde is this worde GOD or this worde LOUE . . . & fasten this worde to thin herte, so that it neuer go thens for thing that bifalleth.[7]

Others write or speak of the penetration of the cloud as something that happens out of the blue, that cannot be commanded. Teresa of Avila was prone to be suddenly taken over by ecstatic visions, though it wasn't something she encouraged or even necessarily welcomed. For ourselves, making time for God as a regular Sabbath discipline is recommended. But in busy lives we can also find 'little Sabbaths' that arrive as gifts – the moments when the blower in the public lavatory is taking longer than we would like to dry our hands; the train is delayed; the queue is long and slow. Thomas Merton said:

> As soon as a man or a woman is fully disposed to be alone with God, they are alone with God no matter where they may be. At that moment they see that though they seem to be in the middle of their journey, they have already arrived at the end. For the life of grace on earth is the beginning of the life of glory. Although they are travellers in time, they have opened their eyes, for a moment, in eternity.[8]

George Herbert thought of God as reserving to himself the gift of true rest for humanity in order to ensure their return to him, if not through desire, then at least through exhaustion:

The Pulley
When God at first made man
Having a glass of blessings standing by,
Let us (said he) pour on him all we can:
Let the world's riches, which dispersed lie,
Contract into a span.

So strength first made a way;
Then beauty flowed, then wisdom, honour,
pleasure:
When almost all was out, God made a stay,
Perceiving that alone of all his treasure
Rest in the bottom lay.

For if I should (said he)
Bestow this jewel also on my creature,
He would adore his gifts in stead of me,
And rest in Nature, not the God of Nature.
So both should losers be.

Yet let him keep the rest
But keep them with repining restlessness:
Let him be rich and weary, that at least,
If goodness lead him not, yet weariness
May toss him to my breast.

George Herbert[9]

Busy lives can hide loneliness and fear. This is as true for the activist seeker after justice as for the workaholic entrepreneur. In a letter, Thomas Merton warned his friend:

> You are probably striving to build yourself an identity in your work and your witness. You are using it to protect yourself against nothingness, annihilation. That is not the right use of your work. All the good that you will do will not come from you but from the fact that you allowed yourself, in the obedience of faith, to be used by God's love. Think of this more and gradually you will be free from the need to prove yourself, and you can be more open to the power that will work through you without your knowing it.[10]

The following poem has worked really well in bringing even large groups of several hundred to stillness, including schoolchildren. It speaks of the flow of Spirit from Ascension to Pentecost as the reader departs, leaving silence behind:

Keeping quiet
Now we will count to twelve
and we will all keep still.

For once on the face of the Earth
let's not speak in any language,
let's stop for one second,
and not move our arms so much.
It would be an exotic moment
without rush, without engines,

we would all be together
in a sudden strangeness.

Fishermen in the cold sea
would not harm whales
and the man gathering salt
would look at his hurt hands.

Those who prepare green wars
wars with gas, wars with fire,
victory with no survivors,
would put on clean clothes
and walk about with their brothers
in the shade, doing nothing.

What I want should not be confused
with total inactivity.
Life is what it is all about;
I want no truck with death.

If we were not so single-minded
about keeping our lives moving
and for once could do nothing,
perhaps a huge silence
might interrupt this sadness
of never understanding ourselves
and of threatening ourselves with death.

Perhaps the Earth can teach us
as when everything seems dead
and later proves to be alive.

Now I'll count up to twelve
and you keep quiet and I will go.

P. Neruda[11]

Re-emerge to praise and serve

But the retreat into the Spirit can never be solipsistic.
Pentecostal spirituality is communal. Having
retreated into stillness and been revitalized,
humanity has to re-emerge into the outer temple,
the phenomenal creation, and serve. It was the role
of the king, and later the priest, to hold all things in
harmony and to restore creation's covenant through
ritual and teaching. The king's justice was seen as
being like the rain that falls on the land and keeps it

fertile: Psalm 72.5–7. Singing God's praise was seen
as joining the music of the angels, and the angels were
seen as embodying the forces of nature: the wind, the
sea, the fire, etc. To sing the praises of God was to help
maintain the creation, and this is still true. With music
we join the harmony of the spheres. In the Eucharistic
prayer we join our song to that of the angels, praising
the God of heaven and earth:

Therefore with angels and archangels
and all the company of heaven,
we proclaim your great and glorious name,
forever praising you and singing

Holy, holy, holy, Lord
God of power and might,
Heaven and earth are full of your glory.
Hosanna in the highest.[12]

As well as teaching the unity of all things and singing
the praise of God to maintain the creation, humanity
re-emerged from the holy of holies is called to 'till and
keep' the land, as the first Adam had been: Genesis
2.15. The Hebrew word *abad*, which is translated as
'till', means literally to serve, and the word *shamar*,
'keep', means to guard or preserve. These are perfectly
appropriate terms to guide our engagement with
creation and our environmental work.

Planting

We should replace the forests. The very special
circumstances that made life possible on the planet
exist because of the interplay between the life growing
on the planet and the atmosphere that surrounds it.
It is a continual exchange of gases between organic
matter and the surrounding air. Trees absorb carbon
dioxide through photosynthesis and pump water back
into the atmosphere. With enough trees, and not too
much carbon dioxide, an efficient interdependent
system helps maintain temperate climates and
fosters life on earth. It isn't only the vast increase
in carbon dioxide in the atmosphere that is causing
global warming; it's also the denuding of the earth's
tree cover to process the carbon dioxide. Serving and

preserving the planet would include preserving her tree cover to ensure that she continued to be fertile.

Composting

As the final part of a series of events called 'Costing the earth? A quest for sustainability', organized by St Paul's Institute, we held a retreat. It was a three-day retreat in the heart of London, with plenty of intellectual and spiritual input, excellent liturgies, music, storytelling, good food and wine, and lots of time for silence. Together we journeyed a long way, to the heights and depths of intellectual enquiry and emotional exploration. At the final session we all spoke out a commitment to follow on from the retreat and lit a candle to signify how seriously we took what we had said. A large percentage of the group said they would start to compost their organic waste.

It seemed such a strangely simple, local thing to do. In a way, following those three days, we felt empowered to change the world and yet all we went away with was a promise to arrange our compost heaps. But tilling and keeping can be as simple and local as that. And with a liturgical understanding of our actions in the world, composting becomes full of meaning. It is where everything organic goes, in a great heap, to warm up and break down and eventually become the rich soil from which all sorts of new life can grow. All the wonderful ideas and new thoughts and better understanding that had come to us during the retreat could be put on the compost, not as an act of throwing away but as an act of reverence: we were preserving without hoarding. Eventually, out of the collection of everything we had learned, new shoots would appear.

Planting trees, composting waste, all give a hand to the revitalizing of the earth promised by the coming of the Holy Spirit at Pentecost.

The world is charged with the grandeur of God.
It will flame out, like shining from shook foil;
It gathers to a greatness, like the ooze of oil
Crushed. Why do men then now not reck his rod?
Generations have trod, have trod, have trod;
And all is seared with trade; bleared, smeared
with toil;
And wears man's smudge and shares man's smell:
the soil
Is bare now, nor can foot feel, being shod.

And for all this, nature is never spent;
There lives the dearest freshness deep down
things;
And though the last lights off the black West went
Oh, morning, at the brown brink eastward,
springs –
Because the Holy Ghost over the bent
World broods with warm breast and with ah!
bright wings.

Gerard Manley Hopkins[13]

LITURGICAL LINKS

For seasonal worship resources for Ascension and Pentecost, see *Common Worship: Times and Seasons* (pages 469–502) and *Together for a Season: Lent, Holy Week and Easter*. Material can also be found in *New Patterns for Worship*, for example, the Thanksgiving for Ascension:

> You, Christ, are the image of the unseen God,
> the firstborn of all creation.
> You created all things in heaven and on earth:
> everything visible and everything invisible,
> thrones, dominions, sovereignties, powers,
> all things were created through you and for you.
> Lord of all creation
> **we worship and adore you.**
>
> You are the radiant light of God's glory:
> you hold all creation together by your word of power.
> Lord of all creation
> **we worship and adore you.**
>
> You are the first to be born from the dead.
> All perfection is found in you,
> and all things were reconciled through you and for you,
> everything in heaven and everything on earth,
> when you made peace by your death on the cross.
> Lord of all creation
> **we worship and adore you.**
>
> The Church is your body,
> you are its head.
> You take your place in heaven
> at the right hand of the divine majesty,
> where we worship and adore you
> with all your creation, singing:
> **Holy, holy, holy Lord,**
> **God of power and might,**
> **heaven and earth are full of your glory.**
> **Hosanna in the highest.**
> **Blessed is he who comes in the name of the Lord.**
> **Hosanna in the highest.** [14]

SERMON POINTS

- A Christian should be like an arrow that is drawn a very long way back into silence and stillness, only to be let fly into the world to travel far and truly in service.
- Silence can be kept in a sermon, too.
- Tilling and keeping were Adam's liturgy; they are ours, too, as second Adams.

Rogationtide, Trinity Sunday and Ordinary Time

Overarching theme:
Extending Christian care to the whole of creation

Practical themes:
• Beating the Bounds
• Leaving a mark
• Millennium yews
• Special flowers
• Churchyards
• Environment Sunday and time for God's creation
• Harvest
• Pets, bats and rushes

Theological themes:
• The Trinity is the essence of dynamic inclusivity

Introduction

In this last section of the book, we mop up the rest of the Christian year with a mixture of practical ideas and meditations.

Practical ideas for Rogationtide

Beating the Bounds

Rogationtide — the three days prior to Ascension Day when Christ returns to glory. Meanwhile, around the parishes, the days of Rogationtide, also known as Gang Days and Holy Thursday, were an opportunity for the clergy and local officials and schoolchildren to join together in walking the parish boundaries, carrying the flower common milkwort. The flowers are blue or white and are shaped like miniature udders: they were probably used as a link with the milk from cattle grazing on milkwort-rich meadows. The walk could include stopping at any oak trees along the way and blessing them with a passage from the Bible. These **Gospel oaks** could still be blessed today for they are not without their problems and many are of a good age. Prayers were said for the 'preservation and multiplying of the fruits of the earth' and were a means of asking for God's blessing on the land, of preserving boundaries, of encouraging fellowship between neighbours through the reconciling of differences, and of charitable giving to the poor. There is an ancient homily for **Beating the Bounds** ceremonies, which paints a picture of country life then and raises many of the issues of rural life now:

Although we be now assembled together, most principally to laud and thank almighty God for his great benefits, by beholding the fields replenished with all manner of fruit, to the maintenance of our corporal necessities, for our food and sustenance; and partly, also to make our humble suits in prayers to his fatherly Providence, to conserve the same fruits in sending us seasonable weather, whereby we may gather in the said fruits, to that end for which his fatherly goodness hath provided them, yet have we occasion secondarily given us in our walks on those days to consider the old ancient bounds and limits belonging to our own township and to other our neighbours bordering about us, to the intent that we should be content with our own, and not contentiously strive for others, to the breach of charity by any encroaching upon another, or claiming one of the other, further than that in ancient right and custom our forefathers have peaceably laid out unto us for our commodity and comfort. And it is the right of every townsman to preserve so much as lieth in him, the liberties, franchises, bounds and limits of his town and country: but to strive for our very rights and duties with the breach of love and charity, which is the only livery of a Christian man, or with the hurt of godly peace and quiet, by which we be knit together in one general fellowship of Christ's family, in one common household of God, that is utterly forbidden. Let us therefore take such heed in maintaining of our bounds and possessions, that we commit not wrong by encroaching upon other. Let us beware of sudden verdict in things of doubt. Let us well advise ourselves to avouch that certainly, either we have no good knowledge or remembrance, or to claim that we have no just title to. Thou shalt not (commandeth almighty God in his law) remove thy neighbour's mark, which they of old time have set in their inheritance. Thou shalt not, saith Solomon, remove the ancient bounds which thy fathers have laid. And lest we should esteem it to be but a light offence so to do, we shall understand that it is reckoned among the curses of God pronounced upon sinners. Accursed be he, saith almighty God by Moses, who removeth his neighbour's doles and marks, and all the people shall say, answering Amen thereto, as ratifying that curse upon whom it doth light. They do much provoke the wrath of God upon themselves, which used to grind up the doles and marks, which of ancient time were laid for the division of meers and balks in the fields, to bring the owners to their right. They do wickedly which do turn up the ancient terres of the fields, that old men beforetimes with great pain did tread out, whereby the lord's records (which be the tenant's evidences) be perverted and translated sometime to the disheriting of the right owner, to the oppression of the poor fatherless or the poor widow. Oh consider, therefore the ire of God against gleaners, gatherers, and encroachers upon other men's lands and possessions! It is lamentable to see in some places how greedy men used to plough and grate upon their neighbour's land that lieth next to them: how covetous men now-a-days plough up so nigh the common baulks and walks, which good men beforetime made the greater

Rogationtide, Trinity Sunday and Ordinary Time

LITURGICAL LINK

Liturgical material for a Rogationtide procession is provided in *Common Worship: Times and Seasons* (pages 614–18).

and broader, partly for commodious walk of his neighbour, partly for the better shack in harvest-time, to the more comfort of his poor neighbour's cattle. It is a shame to behold the insatiableness of some covetous persons in their doings; that where their ancestors left of their land a broad and sufficient bier-balk, to carry the corpse to the Christian sepulcher, how men pinch at such bier-balks, which by long use and custom ought to be inviolably kept for that purpose; and now they quite ear them up, and turn the dead body to be borne farther about in the high streets; or else, if they leave any such meer, it is too strait for two to walk on.[1]

The seventeenth-century poet and preacher George Herbert, rector of Bemerton, Wiltshire, listed the benefits of Beating the Bounds: 'a blessing of God for the fruits of the field; justice in the preservation of bounds; charitie in living walking and neighbourly accompanying one another; mercie in relieving the poor by a liberal distribution of largesse, which at the time is or ought to be used'.[2]

Beating the Bounds was done physically with peeled willow wands. It's yet another fortieth day anniversary, this time the fortieth day after Easter Sunday and the Sunday but one before Whitsun.

Leaving a mark

There were once ceremonies in which an image of Christ was raised to the roof of the church and another image representing the devil as lightning would then be dropped from the roof. It's difficult to see how any of this could encourage environmental

COWSLIP SUNDAY, FIRST SUNDAY IN MAY

According to a Northern European legend, when St Peter was told that duplicate keys to heaven had been made, he let his keys drop on to the ground. Cowslips grew where the keys landed, hence their other name – St Peter's keys.

awareness within our church community today. Perhaps it is an opportunity to come clean and ask what Jesus would do at this time.

If you were about to move on, what changes would you make to leave the world a better place? What would you do to leave your mark?

The tamarisk

In 1582, a former bishop of London left his mark by introducing **tamarisk** to this country. Dr Edmund Grindal was bishop in the time of the first Queen Elizabeth and he brought the plant from the Middle East, where it was known for its medicinal properties. Dr Grindal planted his first tamarisks in his garden at Fulham Palace with the intention of producing a tonic, and of providing a treatment for rheumatism and bruises. Today the good bishop's mark is growing along the east and south coasts and many a coastal walker has been grateful for the way it thrives on salt and sea winds and provides protection along coastal paths.

Yews for the millennium

A project that celebrated the second millennium of the birth of Christ has also left its mark on churchyards throughout the land. **Yews for the Millennium** was organized by The Conservation Foundation as part of its campaign to protect ancient yew trees. No one can be sure exactly how old these ancient trees are, but a method of estimating ages has been used for some, which suggests that some trees could be up to 5,000 years old. The Foundation took cuttings from some of the yews that were estimated to be at least 2,000 years old and invited churches to use these Millennium Yews to help celebrate the year 2000 in a special way –

planting young yews propagated from trees that may well have been alive when Jesus lived on earth. The Millennium Yews were distributed to parishioners at special services, often in cathedrals. Most of the trees were very small, only a few inches high, but now many are several feet tall. Many have plaques recording that they are Millennium Yews and hopefully many will go on to live for a thousand years or more.

If you have a Millennium Yew, start planning a tenth birthday commemoration event as part of the initiative's tenth anniversary, which is being organized by The Conservation Foundation. It's an opportunity to collect photos and mementoes, to gather those who were around ten years ago, and to measure your yew's growth. If your yew did not survive, the Foundation has supplies of replacement yews available.[3]

Is there a special local flower in your churchyard or parish?

Fritillary Sunday is celebrated in St Bartholomew's, Ducklington, near Witney, Oxford. The inside of the church features carvings of fritillaries on pews and pulpit, on a stained-glass window in the vestry and embroidery on the altar cloth and kneelers. A nearby meadow remains unharvested between March and July to allow fritillaries – particularly the snake's head – to flower.

Help for churchyards

Some county Wildlife Trusts, such as the Yorkshire Wildlife Trust, offer help and give advice and awards to churchyards through their Living Churchyards Projects. It has, for instance, produced a Churchyard Management booklet for all the 29 churchyards in the

Howardian Hills Area of Outstanding Beauty. It also organizes visits to churchyards, workshops and seminars.[4] Cornwall's Living Churchyard Scheme monitors vital details on species populations. The scheme assists with management advice, funding, surveys and record keeping for the county's diverse conservation areas and their populations of flora and fauna. This is a wonderful way of enthusing the wider community, especially young people.

CARING FOR GOD'S ACRE

Caring for God's Acre is an independent charity operating over the area of the Hereford Diocese, which covers South Shropshire, Herefordshire, and small areas of Worcestershire, Powys and Gwent. Caring for God's Acre (*www.caringforgodsacre.co.uk*) offers support to community and church groups.

The organization can help with advice and information on churchyard management, assistance with community projects based on churchyards, help with grants and training courses.

Churchyards are very special places because they often contain a rich diversity of plants and animals. They are also important places for archaeology and history, revealing evidence of the past and documenting the lives of people who have lived and worked in the parish.

Grassland is often flower rich and in some cases acts as a refuge for rare or uncommon wildflower and fungi. There may be distinctive and veteran trees of great historical and cultural significance. Churchyard stonework provides a home for a mosaic of mosses and ferns and is a major habitat for lichens; many being rare and only recorded in churchyards. The boundary walls often have fine wall vegetation, having taken years to colonise.

Large and small mammals, birds both resident and summer visitors, insects and butterflies, amphibians and reptiles such as the slow worm find shelter and food within churchyard habitats.

Above all, churchyards provide a focus for community activity and are a peaceful, tranquil place for quiet reflection.

Practical ideas for Trinity Sunday

Trinity could be looked at as a mystery of the threefold nature of the Creator, Restorer and Sustainer. It is said by some that St Patrick used the **shamrock** with its three leaves to illustrate the Trinity. However, the shamrock is as much a mystery as the religious significance of the day. There is much debate about exactly which plant St Patrick would have used for his preaching. The last time people were asked what they believed shamrock to be, over 220 different plants were submitted, with the lesser yellow trefoil winning by a short stem over white clover.

ENVIRONMENT SUNDAY

Environment Sunday, which is celebrated on the Sunday nearest to World Environment Day on 5 June, sometimes falls on Trinity Sunday. There are those who say that every Sunday should be Environment Sunday, but it is good that there are organizations like A Rocha (see Appendix 2: Useful contacts) who are producing worship material, sermon notes, scientific information and practical advice for Christians to become more aware and active in churches, homes and the workplace.

SHEEP SHEARING

In June 2007, history was made at All Saints Church, Cawthorne, when a sheep was sheared and blessed during a service of prayer and thanksgiving for the farming communities of Yorkshire. Local churches are keen to support their local farmers, who have experienced many difficulties over recent years. The service, which was led by the Bishop of Wakefield, focused on thanksgiving for God's gifts in creation and sought to support and encourage farming communities in the region.

LITURGICAL LINK

Common Worship: Times and Seasons provides material for Trinity Sunday (pages 506–13). There are also good resources in *New Patterns for Worship*.

Meditation for Trinity Sunday

Dynamic inclusivity 1: 'I bind myself' meditation

Trinity is the essence of dynamic inclusiveness. The most famous iconic presentation of the Trinity shows the three angels who come to greet Abraham sitting at table with a fourth place in front of them, inviting the observer to sense him or herself sitting with them. The Trinity can also be thought of as a triangle, with one side left undrawn, as if it were an open book, open to gather everything into the dance of interrelationship that the three-in-one, one-in-three manifests.

The hymn *par excellence* that is sung on Trinity Sunday, St Patrick's Breastplate, speaks for itself in terms of engagement with the whole of creation. It is a paean to the cosmic covenant, conveying the sense of everything in creation bound up in the Trinitarian God and in one another.

> I bind unto myself today
> The strong name of the Trinity,
> By invocation of the same,
> The Three in One, and One in Three.
>
> I bind this day to me for ever,
> By power of faith, Christ's Incarnation,
> His baptism in Jordan river;
> His death on Cross for my salvation;
> His bursting forth from the spicèd tomb;
> His riding up the heavenly way;
> His coming at the day of doom;
> I bind unto myself today.
>
> I bind unto myself the power
> Of the great love of Cherubim;
> The sweet 'Well done' in judgement hour;
> The service of the Seraphim,
> Confessors' faith, Apostles' word,

> The Patriarchs' prayers, the Prophets' scrolls,
> All good deeds done unto the Lord,
> And purity of virgin souls.
>
> I bind unto myself today
> The virtues of the star-lit heaven,
> The glorious sun's life-giving ray,
> The whiteness of the moon at even
> The flashing of the lightning free,
> The whirling wind's tempestuous shocks,
> The stable earth, the deep salt sea,
> Around the old eternal rocks.
>
> I bind unto myself today
> The power of God to hold and lead,
> His eye to watch, his might to stay,
> His ear to hearken to my need.
> The wisdom of my God to teach,
> His hand to guide, his shield to ward;
> The word of God to give me speech,
> His heavenly host to be my guard.
>
> Christ be with me, Christ within me,
> Christ behind me, Christ before me,
> Christ beside me, Christ to win me,
> Christ to comfort and restore me.
> Christ beneath me, Christ above me,
> Christ in quiet, Christ in danger,
> Christ in hearts of all who love me,
> Christ in mouth of friend and stranger.
>
> I bind unto myself the name,
> The strong name of the Trinity;
> By invocation of the same,
> The Three in One, and One in Three.
> Of whom all nature hath creation;
> Eternal Father, Spirit, Word:
> Praise to the Lord of my salvation,
> Salvation is of Christ the Lord.[5]

Practical ideas for Ordinary Time

Colour: green

The time in the Christian year from Trinity Sunday to the start of Advent is known as Ordinary Time. It is also known as the time of **'green Sundays'**, green being the liturgical colour of this period.

Lammas Day

Days have been long since Trinity. Summer has been restful, but 1 August sees **Lammas Day** heralding the harvest. The day, also known as the Feast of St Peter ad Vincula, is thought to have been named after the Anglo-Saxon *Loaf-mas*, a celebration of the first bread baked from the new wheat, which is offered for use in the Eucharist. There are other interpretations, such as that it is the day when medieval priests gathered their tithe lambs from the tenants who held lands belonging to the church at York, which is dedicated to St Peter ad Vincula.

Lammas-land (see page 43 above), set aside twice a year, should be heaving with life and goodness.

It has been a tradition for clergymen to record the wonders of the countryside and a beautiful book by Anthony Foottit, who is the fifth generation of his family to be ordained, lovingly describes a host of wild flowers. In *A Gospel of Wild Flowers*, Anthony, sometime Bishop of Lynn, records how our imaginative medieval ancestors glimpsed signs and symbols of their faith in the natural world around them. His writings, together with Pat Albeck's pictures, reopen some of these windows between visible and invisible realities.

Practical ideas for Lammas

Lammas or Loaf-mass could be an excellent time to celebrate all those in the parish who bake their own bread. They could bring their bread to be blessed before being shared – especially to young people who may not normally taste such fare. Others could be encouraged to create corn dollies, or more correctly corn maidens, which could be used for decoration until being returned to the land in the spring.

The Transfiguration

The feast of the **Transfiguration** takes place on 6 August. Jesus is shown to some of his disciples as he truly is: clothed in the light of the *debir*, the holy of holies of the Temple, beyond space and time.[6] The feast of the Transfiguration takes place on the sixth day, which in the first creation story is the day on which Adam was created. So Christ is the second Adam, sacrificing himself on the cross, which becomes the tree of life, undoing the wrong choice made by Adam in Paradise. As 'second Adams' Christians are to till and keep – serve and preserve – the creation:

LITURGICAL LINK

See *Common Worship: Times and Seasons* (pages 621–2) for resources for Lammastide.

CREATION WINDOWS

The unusual orientation of St Chad's Church, Leeds, means that its east window catches the full sunlight, which highlights its creation theme, complete with zebras, flamingos, dolphins, lions and a host of other animals.

If the window is viewed as colour bands, the blue is the creation of the earth, green the garden of Eden and the tree of knowledge, red the sinful earth and the uppermost section introduces the idea of incarnation, with the Holy Spirit in the form of a dove.

The window was created by Margaret Rope, who often signed her work with a picture of a tortoise.

We think that Paradise and Calvary,
Christ's cross and Adam's tree, stood in one place;
Look, Lord, and find both Adams met in me;
As the first Adam's sweat surrounds my face,
May the last Adam's blood my soul embrace.

John Donne[7]

Michaelmas

The **Michaelmas daisy** would seem a natural entry for Anthony's Foottit's book on wild flowers, but it is not considered wild enough, having been introduced here only in the late 1880s. Its name reminds us that the season of Michaelmas is within Ordinary Time.

The Virgin Mary

The feast of the **Nativity of the Blessed Virgin Mary** on 8 September is also significant. The eighth day (in what is the first month of the liturgical year of the Orthodox Church) is the day of the new creation. So Mary, by accepting the birth of Christ in her own body, presages the coming of the new creation in Christ.

TIME FOR GOD'S CREATION

In 1989, the Ecumenical Patriarch invited all Christians to observe 1 September as a day of thanksgiving for the great gift of creation, and an occasion for petitions for its preservation and healing. At the Third European Ecumenical Assembly held in Sibiu (Romania) in 2007, official representatives of the Roman Catholic, Orthodox, Anglican and Protestant Churches made this resolution:

We recommend that the period from the 1st September to the 4th of October be dedicated to prayer for the protection of Creation and the promotion of sustainable lifestyles that reverse our contribution to climate change.

This period concludes with St Francis Day (4 October), on which Roman Catholics increasingly reflect on such themes, and includes the harvest festival, celebrated by Protestant churches. Thus it provides opportunities within most Christian traditions to devote special attention to the confession of God the Father, creator of heaven and earth. The six-week period also gives churches an opportunity for environmental action.

In marking the first article of the Creed, such a celebration deepens our understanding of the seasons of the Christian year from Advent to Pentecost, which reflect the second and third articles (concerning the Incarnation, Passion and Resurrection of Christ and the gift of the Holy Spirit). St Francis Day links it to the cloud of witnesses commemorated in the cycle of saints' days. In these ways, ecological responsibility is related to incarnation, redemption, Eucharist and, indeed, the entirety of our faith.

The Archbishops of Canterbury and York are encouraging all parishes in the Church of England to choose one Sunday between 1 September and the second Sunday in October on which to put creation at the centre of their worship and reflection. Locally, this might be extended to cover a weekend and might be undertaken in cooperation with other churches and, indeed, members of the other Abrahamic faiths. Where appropriate, parishes are encouraged to link their harvest festival celebrations with this celebration, though in some places there will be good reasons for keeping the two occasions separate.

This observance is in addition to the existing reflection on creation, which occurs on the Second Sunday before Lent.

TIME FOR GOD'S CREATION: OLD TESTAMENT READINGS AND PSALMODY

A cosmic hymn of praise	Genesis 1.1 – 2.3
The garden of creation	Genesis 2.4b-19
Creation restored after the deluge	Genesis 8.12-22
God's promise to sustain creation	Genesis 9.8-17
God's provision	Exodus 16.11-15
A feast of fruitfulness	Leviticus 23.33-43
The promise of a fertile land	Leviticus 26.1-13
God's gifts to the redeemed	Deuteronomy 6.9-14
The gift of the land	Deuteronomy 8.7-18
Offering of the first fruits	Deuteronomy 26.1-11
The promise of restoration	Amos 9.13
The covenant of peace with all creation	Hosea 2.18-23
Repentance and restoration	Hosea 14.2-10
The harmony of the animal kingdom in the messianic age	Isaiah 11.1-9
Feasting in God's presence	Isaiah 25.6-9; 55.6-11
The blossoming of the wilderness at God's appearing	Isaiah 35.1-7
A sign of a fruitful future	Jeremiah 32.6-15
God promises his people a peaceable land	Ezekiel 34.25-31
The hope of humankind restored	Ezekiel 37.1-14
A vision of waters restoring the land	Ezekiel 47.6-12
The wonder of creation	Ecclesiasticus 42.15 – 43.12
A garden as symbol of divine love	Song of Songs 4.12-13
Kinship and the land	Ruth 2.1-13
Defiant nature and the hope of immortality	Job 14.7-10
God's majesty and creation's marvel	Job 38.1-11, 16-18
God's wisdom and creation	Proverbs 8.1-4, 22-31
	Psalms: 19; 65; 80; 90.1-6, 13-end; 100; 103; 104.25-37; 106; 107; 112; 126; 136.1-9, 23-26; 146; 147.1-13 (Jubilees 2.21-27)

NEW TESTAMENT READINGS

The Lord of nature brings peace to violent discord	Mark 4.35-41
Nurturing the fig tree	Luke 13.6-9
From the seed to a tree of life – an image of God's reign	Mark 4.30-32 (or, Matthew 13.31-32; Luke 13.18-19)
Hungry people fed on Christ's abundance	John 6.1-13
God's people as a fruitful vine	John 15.1-17
The natural world longing for liberation	Romans 8.18-22
The risen Christ appears in the garden, prefiguring a new creation	John 20.15
Christ as the new creation	Colossians 1.1-15
Creation renewed for the healing of the nations	Revelation 22.1-5
God's generosity and human gratitude	2 Corinthians 9.9-11a
Sufficiency of resources and simplicity of lifestyle	Matthew 6.25-34; 1 Timothy 6.7-10, 17-19
The risen Christ and the abundance of life	John 21.1-14
The promise of Paradise restored	Revelation 2.1-7

HARVEST

Harvest festival at St Bride's, Fleet Street, London, replaces the normal colourful displays of agricultural fruits and flowers with the full-colour front pages of some 300 different newspapers from Britain and around the world: this is the harvest of the printed word with which the church and the area have been famously linked since the fist printing press was established in Fleet Street 500 years ago.

In another part of London, St Andrew's, Fulham Fields, celebrates harvest every week by providing fresh fruit and vegetables regularly to people who otherwise would not get their 'five a day'. Every Tuesday, when in the past the church would have been closed, volunteers – members of the congregation and others – bag up selections of vegetables and salads, which they sell for £2.50. This is tremendous value as each bag contains around 20 items. There is no excess packaging and the food is fresh. Half the customers are non-churchgoers, but since the scheme began Sunday attendances have risen from 70 to 120.

In today's world, where seasons have little relevance to our tables, the celebration of harvest may be questioned. But its relevance today is possibly far greater than it has ever been as it is a means of reconnecting congregations with the land from which their food comes – we still have harvests, despite the appearance of the same food in supermarkets all year round. So it is worth looking at new opportunities to remember the many ways we can bring our harvests home.

Come, ye thankful people, come . . .

Harvest festivals are a major feature of church life at this time. It is strange that, in a Church so steeped in rural life, the festival in the form we know and love is a recent addition, having been created in 1843 by a Victorian vicar in Cornwall. Long before this, however, prayers for a good harvest and thanks for its success would have been a feature of many services.

Church bells would ring every day to encourage those working in the fields around. Often they would work by the light of the **harvest moon**. Perhaps this is another occasion to switch off the floodlighting so that the brightness of the harvest moon can be appreciated for the gift it is to all God's creatures great and small.

The readings and hymns of harvest tend to be upbeat, concentrating on fields and scattering the good seed on the ground, the breezes, the sunshine and the soft, refreshing rain. But harvest has always been adapted to suit communities. Where people combined farming the land with fishing, their reliance on the harvest was two-fold and the men would sing at harvests of the sea services:

LITURGICAL LINK

- Liturgical material for Harvest Thanksgiving is provided in *Common Worship: Times and Seasons* (pages 626–32).
- The feast of **Michael and All Angels**, held on 29 September, can be a time to remember that our sung praises of God join us to music that is already playing: the music of the spheres, the angels sustaining the universe and its forces of wind and weather, earth, fire and life, joining heaven and earth by their song.

'ALL CREATURES GREAT AND SMALL' WELCOMED AT PET SERVICE

On Sunday 14 October, a church in Leeds welcomed 'all creatures great and small' at its first ever pet service. St Paul's Whinmoor, near Seacroft, opened its doors on not only domestic pets, such as cats and dogs, but rabbits, guinea pigs, reptiles and even chickens as part of a pet service inspired by the problems facing the farming industry and the rural community.

Team Vicar of St Paul's, the Revd Clare MacLaren, explained, 'It seemed like a good time of year to have a pet service, as St Francis' Day falls at the beginning of October – and he is remembered for his care and concern for the bird and animal kingdom. I took my chicken Penny along, and thanked God for the lovely eggs she lays.'

The church meets in a primary school at the heart of a Leeds housing estate but the pet service looked out at the concerns of those in rural parts of the diocese of Ripon and Leeds. Before the service, Clare said, 'We will be praying for sheep down south with foot and mouth disease and blue tongue, and for our farmers here in Yorkshire. Even though we're a city parish, we mustn't forget how much we owe to the people and creatures of the countryside.'

Hymns reflecting the animal kingdom were sung, prayers were said, and, in a novel twist to normal services, refreshments after the service were offered not only to owners, but also to the pets.

Our wives and children we commend to thee:
For them we plough the land and plough the deep;
For them by day the golden corn we reap,
By night the silver harvest of the sea.[8]

This meant hard work in those days and, lest we fall for a romantic picture of yesteryear, this is a line from 'Eternal Father, strong to save':

> *O hear us when we cry to thee*
> *for those in peril on the sea.*
>
> William Whiting[9]

BRING YOUR OWN PETS!

New York's cathedral, St John the Divine, has a tradition of welcoming the city's animals to its pews for an annual St Francis service on 4 October. Each year the organizers are amazed at the wide range of wildlife brought in to be blessed.

The world's faiths

In 1986, at the suggestion of HRH Prince Philip, representatives of the five main faiths and leading conservation groups were brought together for the first time. They met at Francistide, in Assisi. Since then this initiative has been nurtured by the Alliance of Religions and Conservation, encouraging the world's faiths to re-establish themselves as leaders of environmental concern.

Lest we forget

All Souls, on 2 November, commemorates all the faithful dead. The festival is said to have originated in the eleventh century, when a Cluniac monk on his way to Jerusalem stopped off at Mount Etna, then supposed by many to be the mouth of hell, and heard voices complaining that the prayers of his fellow monks were helping to release some of the inhabitants. The news greatly impressed the

DAMP-PROOFING WITH RUSHES

In many churches, special services recall the days when the aisles were bare earth and rushes and hay were laid over the floor, both to prevent the aisles turning to mud and to help keep the church warm and dry.

Service dates vary: St Oswald's, Grasmere, holds its Rushbearing Service in the third week of July, and St Mary's and St Michael's, Urswick, on the nearest Sunday to St Michael's Day. In the church at Forest Chapel, near Macclesfield, the service is held on the nearest Sunday to 12 August. Here the rushes are interwoven with marigolds in a way unique to the church. Evensong is at 3 p.m. and the service often has to move outside to accommodate the large congregation.

monk's superior, Abbot Odilon, who immediately declared that every 2 November two prayers should be offered up for all the souls of the faithful departed.

Our environment lacks the drama of Mount Etna, but early November seems the right time to consider not just human death, but the end of much that has been living around us – for everything there is a season, and while the leaves may be dead and lying at our feet, we know that new life will soon bud and early signs will be seen. **Advent** is just a few weeks away!

BATS IN THE BELFRY

One difficulty churches can have involves bats, which, once inside, can cause real problems and use their protected state to resist everything but prayers. The Bat Conservation Trust has a wealth of understanding and contacts around the country (see Appendix 2: Useful contacts).

Appendix 1

Environmental dates

JANUARY

27–28	RSPB Big Garden Birdwatch

FEBRUARY

2	World Wetland Day
3	Potato Day
14–21	National Nest Box Week

MARCH

20	International Earth Day
22	World Water Day
23	Meteorological Day
25–29	Fairtrade Fortnight

APRIL

16	International Noise Awareness Day
18	World Heritage Day
22	Earth Day
26	Walk to Work Day

MAY

6	International Dawn Chorus Day
21	World Day for Cultural Diversity for Dialogue and Development
22	International Day for Biological Diversity
23	Car-free Sunday
29	Royal Oak Day
Throughout May	Walk in the Woods Month

JUNE

5	World Environment Day
7	National Moth Night

| 8 | World Ocean Day |
| 14–22 | National Bike Week |

JULY

| 5 | World Population Day |

AUGUST

9	International Day of the World's Indigenous People
12	Walk to Church Sunday
12	International Youth Day
16	International Day for the Preservation of the Ozone Layer
23 August – 23 October	Seed Gathering Season
28	European Bat Weekend
Last week	World Maritime Day

SEPTEMBER

| 1 September – 2nd Sunday in October | Time for God's Creation |
| 17–18 | Open House Weekend |

OCTOBER

First Monday	World Habitat Day
1	International Day for Older Persons
4–10	World Space Week
5	World Teachers' Day
16	World Food Day
21	Apple Day

NOVEMBER

6	International Day for Preventing the Exploitation of the Environment in War and Armed Conflict
19	World Toilet Day
20	Universal Children's Day
21 November – 6 December	National Tree Week

DECEMBER

| 5 | International Volunteer Day for Economic and Social Development |
| 11 | Mountain Day |

Appendix 2

Useful contacts

Agriculture

Arthur Rank Centre	*www.arthurrankcentre.org.uk*
British Crop Protection Council	*www.bcpc.org*
Crop Protection Association	*www.cropprotection.org.uk*
The Farmer's Conservation Group	*www.tfcg.co.uk*
Farming & Wildlife Advisory Group	*www.fwag.org.uk*
Garden Organic (formerly Henry Doubleday Research Association)	*www.gardenorganic.co.uk*
National Association of Farmers' Markets	*www.farmersmarkets.net*
National Farmers' Union	*www.nfuonline.com*
Soil Association	*www.soilassociation.org*

Birds

Barn Owl Trust	*www.barnowltrust.org.uk*
Birdlife International	*www.birdlife.net*
British Trust for Ornithology	*www.bto.org*
Hawk & Owl Trust	*www.hawkandowl.org*
Royal Society for the Protection of Birds	*www.rspb.org.uk*
Wildfowl & Wetlands Trust	*www.wwt.org.uk*

Campaigning and interested bodies

Aviation Environment Federation	*www.aef.org.uk*
Black Environment Network	*www.ben-network.org.uk*
British Association for the Advancement of Science	*www.the-ba.net/the-ba/*
British Trust for Conservation Volunteers	*www.btcv.org*
Common Ground	*www.commonground.org.uk*
The Conservation Foundation	*www.conservationfoundation.co.uk*
Environmental Investigation Agency	*www.eia-international.org*

Environmental Law Foundation	www.elflaw.org
Friends of the Earth	www.foe.co.uk
Greenpeace	www.greenpeace.org.uk
International Institute for Environment and Development (IIED)	www.iied.org
National Society of Allotments and Leisure Gardeners	www.nsalg.co.uk
Scientists for Global Responsibility	www.sgr.org.uk
Soil Association	www.soilassociation.org
Women's Environmental Network	www.wwf-uk.org
World Wide Fund for Nature	www.wwf.org

Churches, churchyards and burial grounds

The Arbory Trust	www.arborytrust.org
Caring for God's Acre	www.caringforgodsacre.co.uk
Cathedral Fabrics Commission	www.buildingconservation.com
Council for the Care of Churches	www.churchcare.co.uk
The Churches' Conservation Trust	www.visitchurches.org.uk
Friends of Friendless Churches	www.friendsoffriendlesschurches.org.uk
Historic Chapels Trust	www.hct.org.uk
Historic Churches Preservation Trust	www.historicchurches.org.uk

Countryside

Action with Communities in Rural England	www.acre.org.uk
British Association for Shooting & Conservation	www.basc.org.uk
British Grasslands Society	www.britishgrassland.com/bgs/
Council for National Parks	www.cnp.org.uk
Council for the Protection of Rural England	www.cpre.org.uk
Country Landowners Association	www.cla.org.uk
Countryside Alliance	www.countryside.gov.uk
Countryside Restoration Trust	www.livingcountryside.org.uk
Natural England	www.naturalengland.org.uk
Open Spaces Society	www.oss.org.uk

Education

| Field Studies Council | www.field-studies-council.org |

Learning Through Landscapes	www.ltl.org.uk
Wildlife Watch	www.wildlifewatch.org.uk

Energy

Association for the Conservation of Energy	www.ukace.org
Carbon Trust	www.carbonttrust.co.uk
Energy Saving Trust	www.energysavingrust.org.uk
Centre for Alternative Technology	www.cat.org.uk

Faith-based

Alliance of Religions & Conservation	www.arcworld.org
Anglican Communion Environmental Network	www.acen.anglicancommunion.org
A Rocha	www.arocha.org
Christian Aid	www.christian-aid.org
Christian Ecology Link	www.christian-ecology.org.uk
Eco-Congregation	www.ew.ecocongregation.org
Environmental Issues Network	www.ctbi.org.uk
European Christian Environmental Network	www.ecen.org
Interfaith Power and Light	www.theregenerationproject.org
Iona Community	www.iona.org.uk
Islamic Foundation for Ecology and Environmental Sciences	www.ifees.org.uk
John Ray Initiative	www.jri.org.uk
Methodist/URC Environment Network	www.creationchallenge.org.uk
Operation Noah	www.operationnoah.org
Parish Pump Programme	www.conservationfoundation.co.uk
Quakers Living Witness Project	www.livingwitness.org.uk
Religion, Science and the Environment	www.rsesymposia.org
Society of Ordained Scientists	www.thesosc.org
Tearfund	www.tearfund.org

Fauna and flora

Badger Trust	www.badger.org.uk
Bat Conservation Trust	www.bats.org.uk
Botanical Society of the British Isles	www.bsbi.org.uk
British Association of Nature Conservation	www.banc.org.uk
British Beekeepers Association	www.bbka.org.uk

British Deer Society	www.bds.org.uk
British Dragonfly Society	www.dragonflysoc.org
British Ecological Society	www.britishecologicalsociety.org
British Goat Society	www.allgoats.com
British Hedgehog Preservation Society	www.britishhedgehogs.org.uk
British Lichen Society	www.thebls.org.uk
British Naturalists Association	www.bna-naturalist.org
Butterfly Conservation	www.butterfly-conservation.org
Fauna and Flora International	www.fauna-flora.org
Game Conservancy Trust	www.gct.org.uk
Mammal Society	www.abdn.ac.uk/mammal
National Council for the Conservation of Plants and Gardens	www.nccpg.com
Natural England (English Nature)	www.naturalengland.org.uk
The Otter Trust	www.ottertrust.org.uk
People's Trust for Endangered Species	www.ptes.org
Plantlife International	www.plantlife.org.uk
Pond Conservation Trust	www.pondstrust.org.uk
Royal Botanic Gardens	www.kew.org
Royal Horticultural Society	www.rhs.org.uk
The Wild Flower Society	www.thewildflowersociety.com
The Wildlife Trusts	www.wildlifetrusts.org

Government / official

Department of Environment, Transport and the Regions	www.detr.gov.uk
Environment Agency	www.environment-agency.gov.uk
Department for Environment, Food and Rural Affairs	www.defra.gov.uk
Royal Commission on Environmental Pollution	www.rcep.org.uk

Heritage

Architectural Heritage Fund	www.ahfund.org.uk
Crafts Council	www.craftscouncil.org.uk
Embroiderers' Guild	www.embroiderersguild.com
English Heritage	www.english-heritage.org.uk
Folly Fellowship	www.follies.org.uk

The Georgian Group	www.georgiangroup.org.uk
International Council on Monuments & Sites	www.international.icomos.org
Lime Centre	www.thelimecentre.co.uk
The National Trust	www.nationaltrust.org.uk
Society for the Protection of Ancient Buildings	www.spab.org.uk
Victorian Society	www.victorian-society.org.uk

Recycling

Aluminium Packaging & Recycling Organisation	www.alupro.org.uk
Can Makers	www.canmakers.co.uk
Industry Council for Packaging & the Environment	www.incpen.org
Internet Waste Exchange	www.interwaste.co.uk
Recoup Recycling (Plastic bottle recycling)	www.recoup.org/business
Recycle Now	www.recyclenow.com
Steel Can Recycling Information Bureau	www.scrib.org
Textile Recycling Association	www.textile-recycling.org.uk
Tools for Self Reliance	www.tfsr.com
Waste Watch	www.wastewatch.org.uk

Transport

Bicycle Association	www.ba-gb.com
Living Streets (The Pedestrians Association)	www.livingstreets.org.uk
Sustrans	www.sustrans.org.uk

Trees

Ancient Yew Group	www.ancient-yew.org
Arboricultural Association	www.trees.org.uk
British Christmas Tree Growers Association	www.christmastree.org.uk
Forestry Commission	www.forestry.gov.uk
Royal Forestry Society	www.rfs.org.uk
Small Woods Association	www.smallwoods.org.uk
Tree Council	www.treecouncil.org.uk

| Woodland Trust | www.woodland-trust.org.uk |

Urban

British Urban Regeneration Association	www.bura.org.uk
Civic Trust	www.civictrust.org.uk
Groundwork	www.groundwork.org.uk

Water

Inland Waterways Association	www.waterways.org.uk
Marine Conservation Society	www.mcsuk.org
Water Aid	www.wateraid.org.uk

Appendix 3

Example of an environmental policy

Many dioceses of the Church of England have drawn up, or are in the process of developing, environmental policies. Some of the early ones are being reviewed to ensure that they are keeping pace with environmental issues and concerns.

This policy, adopted by the Ripon and Leeds Synod in September 2007, was developed by the Revd Ian White, the Diocesan Environment Officer, and was the result of a fairly lengthy consultation process, beginning before, and continuing at and after, an environment conference held earlier in the year, so lots of people had a chance to comment on drafts, and provide input into the finished document.

As Ian explains, 'The policy draws on many other sources of similar material, such as the 5th Mark of Mission of the Church, and the Policy of the National Church Institutions, as are referred to in the document. Also, using good environmental principles of re-use and re-cycling, the Guidelines section uses some material from other published policies, such as the national policies of the Methodist, Baptist and URC Churches. I also looked at policies from around the Church of England dioceses to help with wording and contents, so my finished document has quite a significant "re-cycled" content, as well as some original stuff.'

Environment Policy for the Diocese of Ripon and Leeds

POLICY STATEMENT

The Diocese affirms its commitment to the 5th Mark of Mission of the Church, which calls upon us 'to strive to safeguard the integrity of creation and sustain and renew the earth'.[1] Through this commitment, the Diocese recognises the need for Christian mission to include a responsibility to love and care for the earth; a duty which has been entrusted to us by God.

The whole of creation belongs to God. The Biblical creation stories affirm the goodness of God's creation, and define the role of humans within creation as one of stewardship, taking on a privileged responsibility of care for the earth and every living creature. The dominion over the earth given to humans is to be understood not as a right to exploit, but to nurture, protect and manage sensitively. We are called to care for the complex and fragile ecology of the earth, while recognising the need for responsible and sustainable development and the pursuit of social justice.[2] The Diocese is, therefore, committed to the ongoing development of theological insights and the practical implications of this understanding of the human role in relation to the earth.

This environment policy provides a framework based upon the above understanding within which we can place our activities within the ongoing life of the Church, including the construction, maintenance and use of church buildings and other church property, and within the individual lifestyles of church members, and this policy is commended for personal and corporate reflection.

The overall objective of this Policy is to promote environmental awareness and active engagement in assessing the environmental impact of all our activities. It invites us to seek to implement ways in which any environmentally damaging impacts of these activities can be minimised or mitigated. The underlying principle is that of sustainability, whereby the needs of the present are met without compromising the ability of future generations to meet their own needs. Recognition must be given to the global dimension of environmental issues, whereby the most damaging effects of environmental degradation are likely to be felt first and most severely by those who have little responsibility for the causes of the damage. We need to think globally and act locally.

In order to help all members of the Diocese translate these basic principles into action, this Policy identifies the following Guidelines, related to specific aspects of the environment and related church activities. It is intended that these Guidelines be adopted by Diocesan bodies, and they are commended to PCCs and individuals as appropriate.

ENVIRONMENT POLICY GUIDELINES

Awareness and commitment
- to promote environmental awareness throughout the Diocese by the adoption of this Policy, its underlying principles and its objectives.
- to encourage the adoption of environment policies at Deanery and Parish level.
- to ensure that Diocesan employees and office holders are familiar with and implement this Environment Policy and its objectives.
- to ensure that Diocesan activities comply with all relevant environmental regulations.

- to encourage study of the scriptures, Christian tradition and environmental issues with subsequent theological and practical reflection, leading to regular thanksgiving for creation, confession of the sin that damages it and prayer for the natural world and for those involved in its use and care.
- to ensure the mission of the church includes proclamation on environmental concerns in line with the living out of the gospel in people's lives, and exercising the prophetic voice of the church in support of appropriate environmental action, such that the views of the church are heard and widely understood.
- to encourage people to calculate their own carbon footprint and to take steps to reduce it.

Energy
- to ensure energy is used efficiently and wherever possible to reduce the amount of energy used.
- to discourage wasteful use of energy in all Diocesan buildings and in people's homes.
- to encourage the increased use of renewable energy, either locally generated or by switching to 'green tariffs'.
- to encourage lifestyles which are less dependent on the burning of fossil fuels.

Water
- to use water carefully and efficiently, seeking the minimisation of wasteful use.
- to adopt water-saving methods where practical and appropriate.
- to avoid pollutants entering the drainage system and soil.

Waste
- to minimise waste production in all areas of activity and aim for a waste-free environment.
- to encourage investment in longer life goods.
- to encourage the re-use, repair and recycling of materials, including the composting of organic matter.
- to dispose of waste in safe and socially responsible ways.

Travel
- to make every effort to reduce the use of car transport by avoidance of unnecessary travel and by making more use of electronic communication systems.
- to encourage the use of more energy efficient vehicles and forms of transport, and to encourage car sharing where possible.
- to encourage adoption of ways of working within church structures that reduces the need for travel, particularly by car, and to encourage use of public transport and travel by bicycle and on foot.
- to support the expansion of good quality public transport and the provision of improved facilities for cyclists and pedestrians.

- to encourage careful consideration of the environmental impact of all journeys made by air.

Materials, resources and procurement
- to aim to purchase goods which minimise the production of material waste, including packaging.
- to take care in the use of all materials and resources to avoid profligacy and minimise wastefulness.
- to maximise the proportion of sustainable materials used, especially wood and paper, and to use recycled materials when this is a viable option.
- to encourage use of locally-made or produced goods and food as far as this is possible and practicable.
- to offer electronic communication as an alternative to paper for those who are suitably equipped.

Buildings, land and the natural environment
- to take into account the 'whole life' costs of materials when repairing, altering and rebuilding premises.
- to build-in maximum energy and water efficiencies into new buildings and to use sustainable building supplies whenever possible.
- to be sensitive to local culture and to use local sources for materials whenever possible.
- to be sensitive to the impact of church activities on the local environment.
- to take appropriate opportunities to conserve and enhance the natural and built environment and to protect habitats for wildlife and biodiversity.

Implementation, monitoring and review

All responsible bodies within the Diocese are invited to give due consideration to this Environment Policy and its Guidelines. A number of individuals, office holders and committees will have responsibilities for implementation and monitoring of effectiveness.

The Diocesan Secretary will be responsible for implementation and monitoring within the Diocesan Office and throughout the administrative activities of the Diocese.

Incumbents, Churchwardens and PCCs are encouraged to take responsibility for implementation at Parish level, and it is recommended that each Parish nominates an individual as their environmental champion who will also act as a point of contact with the Diocesan Environment Officer.

The Housing and Estates Committee in conjunction with the relevant incumbent will be responsible for implementation for clergy housing and other properties owned by the Diocesan Board of Finance.

Guidance on, and monitoring of, implementation will be the responsibility of Archdeacons, the Diocesan Advisory Committee, the Housing and Estates Committee and the Diocesan Environment Officer as appropriate, with an emphasis on the adoption of best environmental practice, and the sharing of best practice ideas throughout the Diocese.

This Environment Policy will be reviewed on a regular basis, and at least every two years, by the Diocesan Environment Officer in conjunction with others as appropriate.

Useful resources

To assist with implementation of this policy at parish level a wide number of resources are available, and the following are particularly to be recommended:

The Eco-congregation Scheme (The Churches Environmental Programme), issued under the auspices of Churches Together in Britain and Ireland, provides an environmental toolkit for local churches. Information can be accessed at **www.ew.ecocongregation.org** and extensive materials can be ordered from details given on the website.

Christian Ecology Link is a multi-denominational UK Christian organisation for people concerned about the Environment. There are many different resources provided via their website at: **www.christian-ecology.org.uk**.

With the adoption of this policy, parishes are provided with a copy of the recent publication, *'How Many Lightbulbs Does It Take To Change A Christian? A Pocket Guide to Shrinking Your Ecological Footprint,'* by Claire Foster & David Shreeve (Church House Publishing, 2007. ISBN 978-071514127-4).

An environmental audit form produced by the Church of England 'Shrinking the Footprint' campaign is also provided for each parish, to enable a simple investigation of current practice and to provide pointers as to how environmental performance could be improved.

Further information can be obtained from the campaign website at: **www.shrinkingthefootprint.cofe.anglican.org**.

Other useful websites include:

Energy

www.roughguides.com/savingenergy

www.carbontrust.co.uk

www.est.org.uk

www.energywatch.org.uk

www.nef.org.uk

www.cse.org.uk

Water

www.waterwise.org.uk

Recycling and Waste

www.recycle-more.co.uk

www.communitycompost.org

Buildings

www.churchcare.co.uk

Appendix 4

Anglican contacts

Diocesan Environment Officers

Every diocese has a Diocesan Environment Officer (DEO). Details can be found on diocesan web sites or from diocesan offices.

Bishop's Environment Group

The current members include the Bishops of London (Chair), Ely, Hulme, Liverpool, Newcastle, Thetford and Wakefield.

Anglican Communion Environment Network

Members represent a number of provinces around the World. Convenor: The Rt Revd George Browning (*gvbrowning@hotmail.com*).

Appendix 5

The Shrinking the Footprint audit

Shrinking the Footprint

MEASURING OUR FOOTPRINT – ENVIRONMENTAL AUDIT

This simple audit will help you assess your church's energy footprint.

Environmental audit

Lighting your church

Is there a need?	Yes	No
Do all the lights need to be on?	Yes	No
Even on a sunny day?	Yes	No
Can all the lights be fitted with energy saving bulbs?	Yes	No
Are all fittings fitted with energy saving bulbs?	Yes	No
Could you use Light Emitting Diodes (LEDs) to illuminate parts of the church and its features?	Yes	No

Exterior lighting –
many churches are floodlit for mission, security, tourism, etc.

Is the timing mechanism adjusted to meet seasonal needs?	Yes	No
Is the illumination programme adjusted to liturgical or individual donors, etc.?	Yes	No
Is the lighting checked regularly to ensure against causing light pollution?	Yes	No
Are energy saving bulbs used?	Yes	No

Heating and insulation

Is the boiler more than 15 years old? (If so then it will probably not be as efficient as it should be)	Yes	No
Is it regularly serviced?	Yes	No
Does it have a time switch?	Yes	No
Is this adjusted to meet seasonal needs?	Yes	No

Is it possible to reduce the heating period?	Yes	No
Are all the windows and doors draught proofed?	Yes	No
Are all pipes lagged?	Yes	No
Are buildings which can be, fitted with roof insulation?	Yes	No
Are cavity walls insulated?	Yes	No
Can parts of the building be heated separately?	Yes	No

Other energy – transport

Is there a car sharing scheme to get people to and from church?	Yes	No
Is there a safe place to leave bicycles?	Yes	No

Record in your Church Log Book the number of energy units used (from your energy bills) and plan to do this at the same time each year.

Remember, all new equipment is likely to cost money initially. The first task for all churches should be to see how the existing facilities can be made more efficient. For more information and resources from the Church of England's national environment campaign, visit **www.shrinkingthefootprint.cofe.anglican.org**.

Notes

INTRODUCTION

1 Claire Foster and David Shreeve, *How Many Lightbulbs Does It Take to Change a Christian? A Pocket Guide to Shrinking your Ecological Footprint*, Church House Publishing. 2007.
2 Gillian Strane and Nathan Oxley, *For Creed and Creation: A simple guidebook for running a greener church*, a booklet produced by The Conservation Foundation in 2007 for the London Church Leaders Group, see *www.shrinking thefootprint. cofe.anglican.org*.
3 Church's Mission and Public Affairs Council, *Sharing God's Planet: A Christian Vision for a Sustainable Future*, Church House Publishing, 2005.
4 See *www.shrinkingthefootprint.cofe.anglican.org*.
5 Jordi Pigem, 'Spiritual Activism', *Resurgence*, Issue 235, March/April 2006.

ADVENT

1 David Stancliffe, *God's Pattern: Shaping our Worship, Ministry and Life*, SPCK, 2003, p. 57.
2 James Lovelock, *The Revenge of Gaia: Why the Earth is Fighting Back, and How We Can Still Save Humanity*, Penguin, 2006.
3 *Common Worship: Times and Seasons*, Church House Publishing, 2006, p.29.
4 As quoted in John Eadie, *The Ecclesiastical Cyclopedia*, Griffin, Bohn & Co., 1862.
5 *Together for a Season: Advent, Christmas and Epiphany*, Church House Publishing, 2006, pp. 57-72.
6 See *www.interfaithpower.org*.
7 David Iliff and John Barnard (compilers), *The Carol Book*, a photocopyiable resource, Royal School of Church Music, 2005.
8 Catherine Keller, 'No more sea: the lost chaos of the eschaton', in D. T. Hessel and R. Radford-Ruether (eds), *Christianity and Ecology: Seeking the Well-Being of Earth and Humans*, Harvard University Press, 2000, pp. 183–98.
9 P. Davies, 'Is the universe a machine?' in Nina Hall (ed.), *Exploring Chaos: A Guide to the New Science of Disorder*, W. W. Norton, 1991, p. 212.
10 L. Winkett, 'Sustainable liturgy', in Claire Foster and Edmund Newell (eds), *Costing the Earth? The Quest for Sustainability*, SCM-Canterbury Press, forthcoming.
11 Keller, *No More Sea*, p. 195.
12 Keller, *No More Sea*, p. 195.

13 Robert Murray, *The Cosmic Covenant: Biblical Themes of Justice, Peace and the Integrity of Creation*, Sheed & Ward, 1992.

14 Murray, *The Cosmic Covenant*.

15 Prayer of Confession from the Iona Community's 'Creation Liturgy', *Iona Abbey Worship Book*, Wild Goose Publications, 2001.

16 *New Patterns for Worship*, Church House Publishing, rev. ed. 2002, B56.

17 Murray, *The Cosmic Covenant*.

18 Naomi Mara Hyman, 'The unmaking of the world', in A. Waskow (ed.), *Torah of the Earth: Exploring 4,000 Years of Ecology in Jewish Thought, vol. 2, Zionism: One Land, Two Peoples*, Jewish Lights Publishing, 2000, pp. 153ff.

19 David S. Toolan, 'Praying in a post-Einsteinian universe', *Cross Currents*, 64:4, Winter 1996–7.

20 Michael Frayn, *Copenhagen*, Methuen Drama, 1998, pp. 71–2.

21 *Common Worship: Services and Prayers for the Church of England: Times and Seasons*, Church House Publishing, 2006.

CHRISTMAS

1 Calvin Dewitt, 'Behemoth and Batrachians in the eye of God: responsibility to other kinds in biblical perspective', in D. T. Hessel and R. Radford-Ruether (eds), *Christianity and Ecology*, Harvard University Press, 2000, p. 302.

2 Margaret Barker, 'Wisdom and the Stewardship of Knowledge', Bishop's Lecture, Lincoln, 2004.

3 See *www.letsrecycle.com*.

4 These are listed on *www.BCTGA.co.uk*.

5 James Lovelock, *The Revenge of Gaia*, Penguin, 2006, p. 19.

6 Anglican Consultative Council, *The Official Report of the Lambeth Conference 1998: Transformation and Renewal*, Morehouse Publishing, 1999, p. 89.

7 Robert Murray, *The Cosmic Covenant*, Sheed & Ward, 1992.

8 Margaret Barker, 'The cosmic covenant', personal notes for a study day.

9 Margaret Barker, *The Great High Priest: The Temple Roots of Christian Liturgy*, T&T Clark, 2003, p.144.

10 Margaret Barker, 'Paradise Lost', in N. Ascherson and A. Marshall (eds), *The Adriatic Sea: A Sea at Risk, a Unity of Purpose,* Religion, Science and the Environment, Athens, 2003. p. 143.

11 Theodore Heibert, 'The Human Vocation', in Hessel and Ruether, *Christianity and Ecology*, pp. 136ff.

12 Barker, 'Wisdom and the Stewardship of Knowledge'.

13 A. Waskow, *Torah of the Earth: Exploring 4,000 Years of Ecology in Jewish Thought, vol. 2*, Jewish Light Publishing, 2000, p. 4.

EPIPHANYTIDE

1   David Stancliffe, *God's Pattern: Shaping our Worship, Ministry and Life*, SPCK, p. 59.
2   *Common Worship: Times and Seasons*, Church House Publishing, 2006, p. 108.
3   *Times and Seasons*, p. 607.
4   *Times and Seasons*, p. 201.
5   For information, contact *ivan@randall.fsnet.co.uk*.
6   See *www.gshp.welwyn.org.uk*.
7   See *www.st-james-picadilly.org* and *www.simondawson.com/index.html*.
8   Margaret Barker, *The Gate of Heaven: History and Symbolism of the Temple in Jerusalem*, SPCK, 1991, p. 70.
9   *Times and Seasons*, p. 163.
10 Barker, *The Gate of Heaven*, p. 30.
11 Barker, *The Gate of Heaven*, p. 65.
12 Margaret Barker, *The Great High Priest*, T&T Clark, 2003, p. 209.
13 C. Bialock, 'I built my house by the sea', quoted in Sheila Cassidy, *Good Friday People*, Darton, Longman & Todd, 1991.
14 Martin Buber, *On the Bible*, p. 126, quoted in A. Waskow (ed.) *Torah of the Earth: Exploring 4,000 Years of Ecology in Jewish Thought, vol. 2*, Jewish Lights Publishing, 2000, p. 35.

LENT

1   Richard Chartres, 'Wisdom, knowledge and information', in N. Ascherson and A. Marshall (eds), *The Adriatic Sea: a Sea at Risk, a Unity of Purpose*, Religion, Science and the Environment, Athens, 2003, pp. 154–5.
2   Tchenka Jane Marion Sunderland, *Walking the Labyrinth*, Tchenka Jane Sunderland, 2004; *tchenka@lineone.net*.
3   Ian Tarrant and Sally Dakin, *Labyrinths and Prayer Stations*, Grove Worship Series W180, Grove Books, 2004.
4   Anthony Foottit , *A Gospel in Wild Flowers*, David & Charles, 2006.
5   This booklet is available from the church.
6   Gillian Ambrose, Peter Craig-Wild, Diane Craven, Peter Moger, *Together for a Season: Lent, Holy Week and Easter*, Church House Publishing, 2006, pp. 34–5.
7   Augustine, *City of God*, Penguin Classics, 2003, 13.24; 12.23.
8   Calvin, *Institutes of the Christian Religion*, Westminster/John Knox Press, 2001, 1.14.22.
9   Lynn White, 'The historical roots of our ecological crisis', *Science*, 155, 10 March 1967, pp. 1203–7.
10 Margaret Barker, comment during retreat presentation, St Katherine's Foundation, London, January 2007.

11 Richard Chartres, *Tree of Knowledge, Tree of Life*, Continuum, 2005, pp. 2–8.

12 Margaret Barker, *The Gate of Heaven*, SPCK, 1991, p. 125.

13 Quoted in Barker, *The Gate of Heaven*, p. 105.

14 Margaret Barker, *The Great High Priest*, p. 211

15 P. Hodgson (ed.), *The Cloud of Unknowing and Related Treatises*, Catholic Records Press, 1982, p. 15.

16 Richard Chartres, *Tree of Knowledge, Tree of Life*, p. 25.

17 Monica Furlong, 'What I Expect of the Clergy'.

HOLY WEEK AND EASTER

1 David Stancliffe, *God's Pattern: Shaping our Worship, Ministry and Life*, SPCK, 2003, p. 72.

2 David Stancliffe, *The Pilgrim Prayerbook: A Manual of Devotion*, Continuum, 2003, p. 147.

3 St John Chrysostom, c. 347–407.

4 Satish Kumar, panellist in 'Does creating wealth cost the earth?' in Claire Foster and Edmund Newell (eds), *Costing the Earth? The Quest for Sustainability*, SCM-Canterbury Press, forthcoming.

5 Martin Warner, *Known to the Senses: Five Days of the Passion*, Continuum, 2004, quoting George Herbert, 'The Invitation'.

6 *Common Worship: Services and Prayers for the Church of England*, Church House Publishing, 2000, p. 291.

7 Warner, *Known to the Senses*, p. 71

8 Jerome, *Commentary on Psalm 135*, quoted Margaret Barker, *The Great High Priest*, T&T Clark, 2003, p. 102.

9 Taken from a thought piece for Three Counties Radio for Good Friday 2006, written and presented by Claire Foster and David Shreeve.

10 Margaret Barker, 'Paradise Lost', in N. Ascherson and A. Marshall (eds), *The Adriatic Sea: A Sea at Risk, a Unity of Purpose*, Religion, Science and the Environment, in association with Text Ltd, Athens, 2003, p. 144.

11 Anon., quoted in *Resurgence*, 227, May/June 2004.

12 I. Skelly, 'The Joy of Silence', *Resurgence*, 228, January/February 2005.

ASCENSION AND PENTECOST

1 David Stancliffe, *God's Pattern: Shaping our Worship, Ministry and Life*, SPCK, 2003, p. 87.

2 Gillian Ambrose, Peter Craig-Wild, Diane Craven, Peter Moger, *Together for a Season: Lent, Holy Week and Easter*, Church House Publishing, p. 123.

3 See *www.arocha.org*.

4   Richard Chartres, 'Wisdom, knowledge and information', N. Ascherson and A. Marshall (eds), *The Adriatic Sea: A Sea at Risk, a Unity of Purpose*, Athens, Religion, Science and the Environment, 2003, p. 156.

5   Margaret Barker, *The Gate of Heaven*, SPCK, 1991, p. 102.

6   D. H. Lawrence, 'Shadows'.

7   P. Hodgson (ed.), *The Cloud of Unknowing and Related Treatises*, Catholic Records Press, 1982, p. 14.

8   Thomas Merton, *Thoughts in Solitude*, Burns and Oates, 1958, p. 81.

9   George Herbert, 'The Pulley'.

10 Thomas Merton, 'Letter to James Forest, Feb. 21, 1965', in C. Bochen (ed.) *Essential Writings*, Orbis Books, 2001, pp. 135–6.

11 P. Neruda, 'Keeping Quiet', quoted in *Resurgence*, Issue 233, Nov./Dec., 2005.

12 Short Proper Preface and Sanctus from *Common Worship: Services and Prayers for the Church of England*, Church House Publishing, 2000, p. 176.

13 Gerard Manley Hopkins, 'God's Grandeur', in D. H. S. Nicholson and A. H. E. Lee (eds), *The Oxford Book of Mystical Verse*, Clarendon Press, 1917.

14 *New Patterns for Worship*, Church House Publishing, rev. ed. 2002, G66.

ROGATIONTIDE, TRINITY SUNDAY, ORDINARY TIME

1   See John Edie, *The Ecclesiastical Cyclopaedia*, Griffin, Bohn & Co., 1862.

2   George Herbert, *A Priest to the Temple*, 1652.

3   See *info@conservationfoundation.co.uk*.

4   Contact Elizabeth Hardcastle at *elizabeth.hardcastle@ywt.org.uk*.

5   St Patrick (372–466), translated by Mrs C. F. Alexander (1818–1895).

6   Margaret Barker, *Great High Priest*, London, T&T Clark, p. 186.

7   John Donne, from 'Hymn to God, My God in my Sickness' in James Russell Lowell (ed.), *The Poems of John Donne*, Grolier Club, 1895.

8   'The Manx Fisherman's Evening Hymn', based on a prayer in the *Manx Book of Common Prayer*. It appeared in *The Manx Song Book* in 1896.

9   William Whiting of Winchester, from 'Eternal Father, strong to save', 1860.

APPENDIX 3

1   Adopted by the Bishops of the Lambeth Conference in 1988 and by the General Synod of the Church of England in 1996.

2   This is in line with the Environmental Policy of the National Church Institutions of the Church of England.

Bibliography

ENVIRONMENTAL TITLES

Church's Mission and Public Affairs Council, *Sharing God's Planet: A Christian Vision for a Sustainable Future*, Church House Publishing, 2005

Claire Foster and Edmund Newell (eds), *Costing the Earth? The Quest for Sustainability*, SCM-Canterbury Press, forthcoming

Claire Foster and David Shreeve, *How Many Lightbulbs Does It Take to Change a Christian? A Pocket Guide to Shrinking Your Ecological Footprint*, Church House Publishing, 2007

M. Frayn, *Copenhagen*, Methuen Drama, 1998

Nina Hall (ed.), *Exploring Chaos: A Guide to the New Science of Disorder*, W. W. Norton, 1992

James Lovelock, *The Revenge of Gaia: Why the Earth is Fighting Back, and How We Can Still Save Humanity*, Penguin Books, 2007

Gillian Straine and Nathan Oxley, *For Creed and Creation: A Simple Guidebook for Running a Greener Church*, a booklet produced by The Conservation Foundation for the London Church Leaders Group, 2007

GENERAL TITLES

Sheila Cassidy, *Good Friday People*, Darton, Longman & Todd, 1991

Anthony Foottit, *A Gospel of Wild Flowers*, David & Charles, 2006

David Iliff and John Barnard (eds), *The Carol Book*, Royal School of Church Music, 2005

D. H. S. Nicholson and A. H. E. Lee (eds), *The Oxford Book of Mystical Verse*, Clarendon Press, 1917

Mary Oliver, *New and Selected Poems*, Beacon Press, 1992

LITURGICAL TITLES

Gillian Ambrose, Peter Craig-Wild, Diane Craven and Mary Hawes,
Together for a Season: All-Age Seasonal Material for Advent, Christmas and Epiphany, Church House Publishing, 2006

Gillian Ambrose, Peter Craig-Wild, Diane Craven and Peter Moger,
Together for a Season: Lent, Holy Week and Easter, Church House Publishing, 2007

Common Worship: Services and Prayers for the Church of England,
Church House Publishing, 2000

Common Worship: Additional Collects, Church House Publishing, 2004

Common Worship: Christian Initiation, Church House Publishing, 2005

Common Worship: Times and Seasons, Church House Publishing, 2006

David Kennedy, *Using Common Worship: Times and Seasons: All Saints to Candlemas*,
Church House Publishing 2006

New Patterns for Worship, Church House Publishing, rev. ed., 2002

David Stancliffe, *God's Pattern: Shaping our Worship, Ministry and Life*, SPCK, 2003

David Stancliffe, *The Pilgrim Prayer Book: A Manual of Devotion*, Continuum, 2003

tchenka Jane Marian Sunderland, *Walking the Labyrinth*, Jane Sunderland, 2004

Ian Tarrant and Sally Dakin, *Labyrinths and Prayer Stations*, Grove Worship Series
W180, Grove Books, 2004

THEOLOGICAL TITLES

Anglican Consultative Council, *The Official Report of the Lambeth Conference, 1998: Transformation and Renewal*, Continuum, 1999

N. Ascherson and A. Marshall (eds), *The Adriatic Sea: A Sea at Risk, a Unity of Purpose*, Religion, Science and the Environment, in association with Text Ltd, Athens, 2003

Augustine, *City of God*, Penguin Classics, 2003

Margaret Barker, *The Gate of Heaven: History and Symbolism of the Temple in Jerusalem*, SPCK, 1991

Margaret Barker, *The Great High Priest: The Temple Roots of Christian Liturgy*, T&T Clark, 2003

Christine M. Bochen (ed.), *Thomas Merton: Essential Writings*, Orbis Books, 2000

Calvin, *Institutes of the Christian Religion*, Westminster/John Knox Press, 2001

Richard Chartres, *Tree of Knowledge, Tree of Life*, Continuum, 2005

Church's Mission and Public Affairs Council, *Sharing God's Planet: A Christian Vision for a Sustainable Future*, Church House Publishing, 2005

John Eadie, *The Ecclesiastical Cyclopaedia*, Griffin, Bohn & Co., 1862

D. T. Hessel and R. Radford-Ruether (eds), *Christianity and Ecology: Seeking the Well-being of Earth and Humans*, Harvard University Press, 2000

Hodgson, P. (ed.), *The Cloud of Unknowing and Related Treatises*, Catholic Records Press, 1982

Thomas Merton, *Thoughts in Solitude*, Burns & Oates, 1958

Robert Murray, *The Cosmic Covenant: Biblical Themes of Justice, Peace and the Integrity of Creation*, Sheed & Ward, 1992

Martin Warner, *Known to the Senses: Five Days of the Passion*, Continuum, 2004

A. Waskow (ed.), *Torah of the Earth: Exploring 4,000 years of Ecology in Jewish Thought, vol. 2, Zionism: One Land, Two Peoples; Eco-Judaism: One Earth, Many Peoples*, Jewish Lights Publishing, 2000

General index

Index of biblical references